THE SOUTHERN GARDEN

Admittance
five dollar donation

THE SOUTHERN GARDEN

LYDIA LONGSHORE
WITH THE EDITORS OF Southern Accents

BULFINCH PRESS

NEW YORK · BOSTON

Copyright © 2001 by Southern Accents Magazine

Bulfinch Press

Time Warner Book Group
1271 Avenue of the Americas
New York, NY 10020
Visit our Web site at www.bulfinchpress.com

First paperback edition: April 2006

Library of Congress Cataloging-in-Publication Data
Longshore, Lydia.
    The southern garden / Lydia Longshore
with the editors of Southern Accents.— 1st ed.
        p. cm.
    ISBN 0-8212-2744-0 (hc) / 0-8212-5775-7 (pb)
    1. Gardening—Southern States. 2. Gardens—
Southern States. I. Southern accents. II. Title.
SB453.2S66 L66 2001
635'.0975—dc21   2001025351

Picture credits appear on page 191.

Design by Tom Morgan, Blue Design

Printed in China

Pages 2–3: A statue of Flora beckons from the end of a pleached crab apple allée at Glen Burnie, Winchester, Virginia.

Page 4: The gate of Ryan Gainey's Atlanta garden is a splendid example of cottage garden architecture.

Right: Peeling paint and slightly worn objects fit in perfectly in Becky Thompson's Little Rock, Arkansas, cottage garden.

Page 8: A banana leaf with its generous dimensions adds tropical flair to Peggy Sewell's Dallas garden.

Pages 10–11: Round boxwoods create a sense of rhythm and anticipation on the approach to this front door in Nashville, Tennessee.

CONTENTS

INTRODUCTION

Ralph Waldo Emerson wrote: "A garden is like one of those pernicious machineries which catch a man's coat-skirt or his hand, draw in his arm, his leg and his whole body to irresistible destruction."

I don't know why I love gardening. There are so many perils along with the well-documented rewards shown in the pages of Southern Accents. There are insects and disease and flood and drought. In fact, as I worked on this book in the summer of 2000, Alabama experienced its worst

Opposite: A garden is at once for display and essentially private, like this one that lies beyond an enticing doorway. **Above:** A thoughtful female figure studies her garden domain.

13

drought in years. It didn't rain from June until October. We were subject to water restrictions, and I and many others went to great lengths to water our gardens — saving my children's bathwater, for instance, and toting it downstairs to water my roses by the bucketful. I fear some of the summer's disappointment seeped into the text, even though I tried to focus on the images of perfect gardens we've shown in *Southern Accents*. Oddly enough, many of my plants survived, and I learned that they didn't need the daily watering I had treated them to

prior to the drought. I know they are stronger now, with more vigorous roots and an ability to survive on their own.

Like all gardening lessons, this one had reverberations in my own life. When I went through a divorce, I threw myself into the garden, trying to bring order and beauty to the bleakest of domestic moments. In my new home, trying to create a stable family life for my children, I planted my tiny yard with only my favorite plants, setting down roots, trying to bloom. Some flourished, others faltered. My sedum, which had thrived in previous gardens, died altogether, something I found especially disheartening. And yet we survived the drought. My buddleia is gorgeous, roses fill vases in my house all summer long, and I can cook nearly anything with the herbs outside my kitchen door. I tended my garden, and my garden nourished me right back, reassuring me that I could rebuild my life, that I could establish structure, that I could provide.

I believe that cooking and gardening are closely connected and that if you love one, you probably love the other. I have always loved both, to an unreasonable degree. The thing I miss most about married life is having someone to cook for. Even in our darkest days, I prepared osso bucco for my husband, although we ate in stony silence. The advantage of gardening is that you can do it solely for your own pleasure. And by and large, gardening is a solitary pursuit.

Opposite: 'Eden,' a climbing rose, is cherished for its tight, delicate pink blossoms. **Above:** Dense plantings, broken by artfully arranged stones and a cascading rivulet, create a fairy-tale atmosphere in Donna Hackman's Virginia wonderland.

15

Opposite: In Birmingham, Alabama, the afternoon sunshine bathes a hillside garden in golden light. Right: Hollyhocks form the signature statement of George "Frolic" Weymouth's fantastical Delaware garden.

I was an only child until I was seven years old. Growing up on a hillside in Birmingham, I saw few children in my neighborhood, and the houses didn't lend themselves to neighborly interaction. Instead, I lived in our big yard, ranging over three terraces carved into the hillside. On the upper level, azaleas and dog-woods made a woodland garden, where we buried a succession of beloved dogs, cats, and a few fish. At the street, English ivy covered a steep slope. But near the house, in the central section, I found a world of miniature miracles.

In the spring, the crocuses would appear suddenly, their juicy purple buds promising all sorts of robust flowering. I made it my mission to clear detritus from around the shoots, willing the buds open with all the fervent enthusiasm of a nascent gardener. A stash of oyster shells, probably from some previous owner's oyster roast, that I discovered under the ivy became homes for roly-polies when I lined them with moss. I always assumed the shells were left behind when the ocean receded from the land, a notion I did not question until I was embar-rassingly old. With exacting scrutiny, I combed every inch of the garden, examining the plants in minute detail, filled with the marvelous immediacy of each branch and leaf.

I was possessed of a boundless enthusiasm for yard work, wearing my hands down to blisters and dismaying the few friends I invited over to share in the fun. I would help my father rake leaves wearing only my eyelet-edged underpants, in my view perfectly equivalent to Daddy's shirtless work attire. Though today I dress more appropriately for gardening, I still have an unreasonable fondness for the unpleasant tasks of maintenance. Weeding, raking, pruning — heaven.

Which is why I particularly admire the gardeners we feature in *Southern Accents*. They don't take shortcuts. They don't look for low-maintenance solutions to gardening's dilemmas. When a hurricane comes along and wipes out forty-five rosebushes, they go right out and buy sixty new ones. When one area of their vast estate is perfect, they turn to the next acre. They are especially hard to reach by phone, because they are always in the garden. And when they're in the house, I know exactly what they're doing — they're cooking.

The pleasures of home life come not through what we acquire and how we display it. Gratification comes rather through the tasks we've accomplished, the environment we've created, the drought endured.

CHAPTER ONE

FORMAL GARDENS

*I*n the grand estates and tidy town homes of southern cities, a formal style of garden holds firm to its position as the South's favorite form of garden design. Epitomized by the rigorous geometrics and symmetry established by the great French landscape architect André Le Nôtre at the palaces of Versailles and Vaux-le-Vicomte, the style of garden favored by the monarchs of France and Italy seems especially at home in the kingdoms of southern gardeners. The carefully laid out beds arranged on axes,

Opposite: Looking from the house, the axis works its magic to draw the eye to the gate at the garden's edge in this Palm Beach garden. **Above:** A putti fountain at Tyreconnell in Baltimore, Maryland, invites the visitor to take a moment of rest and contemplation before ascending the steep staircase.

19

Below left: Azaleas in profuse bloom welcome visitors to the walled garden. Below right: Beds of tulips and heather surround classical statuary of the Four Seasons. Opposite: Glimpsed through an archway, the substantial walls and statuary establish boundaries between the house and the surrounding gardens.

with their long vistas and organized plantings, are at once playful and serious, as profound and contradictory as the southern character.

From about 1500 B.C., formal gardening has existed, mainly by necessity. Medicinal herbs, which we know were grown by the Sumerians in the third millennium B.C., had to be planted in neat rows and squares to allow for tending and harvesting. Anthony Huxley, author of *An Illustrated History of Gardening*, claims that "man has an innate sense of formality" and goes on to support that notion with plentiful examples of very early formal arrangements of vegetables and herbs. Greece and Rome laid the models for formal garden design, which later societies adopted in Renaissance Europe from the fourteenth to the seventeenth centuries. Certainly

southerners have always embraced classical design, whether in their love of Napoleonic motifs in antiques or in neoclassical architecture for their homes. The stereotypical image of the southern home is the columned Greek Revival facade of Tara, a standard that is alive and well even in new construction. And the type of garden that most reflects those classical ideals is the formal garden, with its flush angles and satisfying symmetry. But unlike the formal gardens of the past, or like the best of them, southern formal gardens reveal a sense of joy and an appreciation for frivolity.

The great southern garden writer Elizabeth Lawrence stated in her 1942 book *A Southern Garden* that the formal garden is perfectly adapted for the southern climate: "I often wish that I had not inherited my garden as it is, in the English tradition of perennial borders and

turf (so-called) and forest trees. I think if I were beginning anew I would like to lay it out in the manner of gardens in Southern France, in a formal pattern of shrubs and pebbled squares enclosed by walls and shaded by lindens: the sort of garden that is made for hot weather by wise people who adapt themselves to their surroundings."

The highly ordered formal style suits the way southerners like to live. Since outdoor spaces are also used for living and entertaining, the garden does more than provide pretty views from the house's windows. It is a place of interaction, an arena for contact, both with members of our own species and with the plant kingdom we cultivate. In our southern climate, which allows us to spend so much time out-doors, the garden is an integral part of the home. We have great traditions of porches and

terraces to bridge the gap between house and garden. The garden is a place we use for entertaining, for lunches in the springtime, for cocktail suppers and dancing in the summer, for solitary meditation, and for many of life's simple pleasures, like breakfast among the azaleas. Emily Whaley, in the charming book she wrote with William P. Baldwin, *Mrs. Whaley and Her Charleston Garden*, says that she cherished the hours she spent alone in a secret space in her garden:

"I come here in the morning, still in my nightgown, to drink my coffee. I look down the way and see my rocky fountain and the little terra-cotta fox. My imagination goes on and on. A lot of the time I think this garden is complete and then I realize it could be better and the next day I'm starting over."

Whaley is also eloquent in her description of a

24

Opposite: Near the house at Glen Burnie, a classical bust is framed by a pair of spiral box topiary. **Below:** The perennial gardens at Glen Burnie burst with a profusion of color. Some of the plants there include pennisetum, purple coneflower, bee balm, yarrow, and liatris.

garden's place in the natural order: "Aunt Em said a garden should be enclosed. She said a garden pushed back the wilderness. A garden was an intimate ground safe from lions and elephants and whatever else was out there." In his *The Inviting Garden*, the great garden writer Allen Lacy, a native of Texas, says that "a garden is not 'natural' in the pure sense of the word." Lacy goes on to note that gardening is rather the demonstration of mankind's skill at taming nature, bending and shaping it with our abilities and imaginations. It is, in fact, the expression of nature filtered through the human experience. The formal garden is surely an exercise in proving our control over the natural world. Left to its own devices, that neatly trimmed garden would most certainly revert to bramble, weeds, or merely a scrubby meadow. With our help, and generous applications of fertilizers, pruning shears, and, if you're chemically inclined, pesticides, plants can be coaxed to flourish where they might otherwise fall victim to drought, insects, and murderous neighboring plants.

Anyone who has ever sold a house and then driven by over the months as the new owners let the garden fall into ruin knows the amazing rapidity with which nature reclaims her own. There is no heartbreak like the inexorable decline of a garden you've poured your heart and wallet into. The edges blur first, then the blackspot denudes your roses, and finally the oleander you coddled with blankets over the

cold spell withers and dies. By the next season, all is lost, the evidence of your passion overrun with indifferent weeds. In fact, one special southern garden was reclaimed from just that sort of landscape gone wild. Surrounding a historic house in Winchester, Virginia, the gardens of Glen Burnie were built out of a near wasteland of property. As Glen Burnie's late curator Lee Taylor described it, "Cows were grazing in the front yard, and maybe a couple of times through the hall." Over the years, the family had moved away and allowed the property to fall into decline.

Visit Glen Burnie today, tucked into the bucolic Shenandoah Valley, and you'll find a scene straight out of a Merchant Ivory movie, with the livestock locked firmly in the pasture.

Opposite: A statue of Mercury salutes the mammoth boxwood beyond.
Above: At Glen Burnie, woodland, water gardens, and formal gardens
spread out across the property. In a classic parterre at the southern side of
the house, the formal patterns of shrubbery focus the eye on the central
statue of Mercury.

Left: Glen Burnie's signature formal vista is the statue of Flora at the end of a pleached crab apple allée. **Opposite:** A loosely planted parterre near the edge of Glen Burnie's cultivated property suggests the wilderness beyond the hedges.

The 250-acre estate was home to a surveyor, Colonel James Wood, who built the first structure, probably a log cabin, about 1738, on the site of the existing Georgian house. He also founded the town of Winchester. The last family member to occupy the house, Julian Wood Glass Jr., initiated its restoration in the 1950s. It was he who established the gardens, planning them in an eighteenth-century style. Sharply defined garden rooms unfold around the house, mapped out, delineated, and charmingly individual. There, even the vegetable garden is planted in patterns, with lettuces, thirty-year-old asparagus, and even the notoriously independent tomato plants laid out for looks rather than function.

The most notable element of formality at Glen Burnie is the striking pleached crab apple allée, with its statue of Flora at the far end, drawing the eye down the axis. Its classical formality touches everyone who passes through it; it is the most-photographed element of the garden. With a typically southern flourish, the gardeners place bouquets of flowers in Flora's arms on special occasions.

Lee Taylor designed the parterre garden in 1962 by drawing a chalk outline of the garden's angles on the ground. A surprise snow that night erased his design, and he had to start over in the morning. Today the neatly trimmed boxwoods set the stage for the dramatic centerpiece statue of Mercury. Pruned in tiers, the shrubs in contrasting colors of chartreuse, rust, and green build in height to frame the graceful statue. At the far corners, giant orbs of boxwoods seem to stand guard.

The axial alignment of formal gardens distinguishes them from the more naturally

flowing country style. At Glen Burnie, the main gardens are located behind the house. From the back entrance, the grand allée of crab apple trees runs to the family cemetery, which holds the twenty-three marked graves of the Woods and Glasses who occupied Glen Burnie, as well as that of Lee Taylor. To the north of the allée, the formal vegetable gardens and the herb garden spread out near the old guest quarters. The rose garden and perennial garden open in succession to the south of the allée, providing a heady experience of color and fragrance. Through an opening in a hedge, you step into a sculpture garden completely enclosed by eight-foot-tall hedges of Hatfield yews. From a bird's-eye view, the entire grounds can be seen to spread out in a clear grid. As an extension of the house, Glen Burnie's gardens allow you to walk from the doorway to the property line with a full sense of the character of the men who created the place out of a former cow pasture.

A wilderness of a different sort faces Patsy and Jack Holden at their Creole garden at Maison Chenal, their home in New Iberia, Louisiana. The savage weather and rich alluvion soil create an environment that rewards the most ruthless plants and punishes the arrogant gardener. Adaptability is all, when one plant insists on taking root and flourishing while its neighbor withers. It is a strange Darwinian balance, more akin to Africa, where periods of jungle moisture alternate with

Opposite: The vast size of the live oak at Maison Chenal inspires awe. **Above, top:** An urn lends Italianate elegance to the parterre garden. **Above, bottom:** At Patsy and Jack Holden's restored farmhouse in Louisiana, the vegetable garden gets formal treatment, down to the pea gravel paths separating the beds.

Below: The formal rose garden at Maison Chenal provides stark contrast to the utilitarian spirit of the working farm. **Opposite:** In the fog, the *pigeonnier* has a timeless romance.

blistering droughts. Only the strong would be expected to survive, but this land is also full of surprises, like the delicate but amazingly tough native lantana.

Patsy Holden insists on calling her garden Creole, in tribute to its French underpinnings filtered through the Louisiana imagination. "It's a product of this climate and this place," says Patsy. As Patrick Dunne, a *Southern Accents* contributor, wrote of her garden: "They had to determine how to impose order on an unruly nature, how to express a French sense of

civilization in a tropical climate that resents all borders and rules, and, especially, how to coax the plants loved by old-world gardeners to coexist with the exotic, even savage ones native to this vibrant soil that has its own rhythm and rage." The Holdens' formal garden is defined by hedges of privet, separated by pea gravel paths. Inside that framework, antique roses, balsam, and even pineapples flourish.

The Holdens brought to their property several nineteenth-century dependencies — a *pigeonnier*, beehives, a chicken house, and a kitchen, which they placed on axes around the main house. It is surely one of the most inventive uses of the formal garden plan, this classically minded working farm. Chickens run in the yard, along with the occasional turkey, while indigo and lantana spill from the parterre borders, blurring the rigid lines. Old roses, some grown from cuttings found in the ruins of the nearby plantation Wartelle House, contribute their ruffled beauty near a vigorous muscadine vine, in the animated dialogue of Old World and New.

Another gardener who takes her inspiration from European garden design but makes it her own lives in Charlottesville, Virginia. There, in a bucolic setting with views of the Blue Ridge Mountains in the distance, she lives with her husband and children in a brick house surrounded by pastures where Limousin cattle and horses graze and gallop. Using the grounds near the house as her laboratory, the gardener began

Left: A table set under the pergola permits entertaining in the center of the garden. Opposite: At Tyreconnell, a striking stone staircase descends the wooded hillside site. The garden was inspired by the fountains and gardens at the Villa d'Este in Tivoli, Italy.

experimenting with garden design by laying out her garden room by room in a formal pattern. The end result is a garden that is not only a great accomplishment but also a living time line of a gardener's growth.

First the owner recognized the need for demarcation between the garden and the surrounding fields. "I wanted some kind of enclosure and definition. Structure was extraordinarily important to help get the sense of theater I was hoping for," she says. She ordered that walls be built, using salvaged brick to blend in with the house, and incorporated a gazebo for easy outdoor enjoyment. Sitting at one end of the parterre axis, the gazebo serves to anchor the vista at one end, while a simple white garden bench stops the eye at the other.

Interestingly enough, the only existing garden element on the property when the new

owners moved in was a neglected parterre, bravely holding the fort of formality against the surrounding pastures. The gardener's first act was to restore the parterre's crisp definition. And then she began her horticultural education, starting with a simple oblong of grass and boxwood that the family calls the Quiet Garden. Next she ventured into color in the Yellow Garden. Over the years, she created new garden rooms and explored new garden passions, like a rose garden and an Orange Garden of dahlias, butterfly weed, viburnum, and daylilies. And as she has matured, the garden reflects those changes, too, like the blue that she introduced into the Yellow Garden when she grew more confident with color combinations. The different gardens unfold in a series of rooms: some divided into wedges with low boxwoods and pathways of pea gravel, others threaded with grassy paths between the dramatic curves of full beds.

Also taking its inspiration from the Old World, the garden at Tyreconnell, in Baltimore, Maryland, pays tribute to the magnificent sixteenth-century garden at Villa d'Este, in Tivoli, Italy. Situated on a hilly twenty-two-acre estate, the garden has as its most striking feature a quarter-mile-long slate staircase descending from the house, crossing a bridge, and climbing a neighboring hillside. In the 1920s, Mr. and Mrs. John Sears Gibbs Jr. hired Arthur Folsom Paul, a fledgling landscape architect recently graduated from the newly

Opposite: A pair of box-edged beds flanks a majestic kapok tree.
Right: The graceful shape of the quatrefoil pool permits a pause before further exploration of the garden.

established program at Harvard, to re-create the Italian garden they loved. Paul took the principles at work in the Villa d'Este gardens and applied them to the Maryland site. He preserved the old woodland and laid out the garden in connected rooms, always mindful of the views of distant hills. In this dramatic garden, the long vistas are framed by the house at one end, and a fountain at the other.

Terraces wrap three sides of the house and provide transition down to lower gardens, each with its own personality and story. On the western terrace, a sunken pool and urn planters lend Italianate grace. An adjacent lawn leads you through groves of trees to the surprising view of Lake Roland. The amazing staircase provides a vista that is three-dimensional, with the stones marching not just off into the distance but steeply downhill and up the next

slope. Near the house, formal flower gardens of azaleas and tulips, surrounded by stone walls, give way to an admiration for the natural beauty of the place as you move away from the house. As the natural beauty grows in grandeur, with the hills in the distance and the lake below, the touch of the gardener grows less evident and gradually ends.

In Palm Beach, where most properties are surrounded by walls and where formality in everything from dress to entertaining flourishes, the formal garden reaches a tropical apotheosis. The landscape architecture firm Sanchez & Maddux specializes in just the sort of French-inspired plan that seems at home on the exclusive island. Behind the tall ficus hedges and the pristine stucco walls, you are likely to find spaces divided by hedges, usually featuring a swimming pool and presenting you

Opposite: The clipped, manicured gardens of Palm Beach lend themselves to a formal style. Here at a grand estate designed by Jorge Sanchez, the eye is drawn down a powerful vista toward the pool and house beyond.

with the strong axes and symmetry of formal garden design.

At Robert and Wendy Meister's lakefront estate in Palm Beach, Jorge Sanchez took on the restoration of gardens that had grown into a tangle over fifty years of neglect. John Volk had designed the original gardens in 1938. Since then, however, they had been allowed to grow unchecked. The gardens feature a kapok tree more than a hundred years old, the largest of four landmarked trees on the island, and two allées of palm trees. In the eighteen-month restoration project, Sanchez sought to retain what worked of Volk's original design, like the avenue of areca palms leading to a grand circular fountain. The peaceful atmosphere engendered by the enclosed space and splash of water lends an air of privacy and intimacy to the area. But Sanchez also wanted his garden to reflect the lives of the current owners, who are firmly rooted in the twenty-first century. He added more tropical plants, specifically chosen to require less maintenance. In rearranging the areca palms, transplanting more than a hundred, he formed two allées, each with a different character but both based on the Italian model of cypress allées. On both allées, Sanchez established dramatic vistas, such as the view from the pool house over the pool and continuing across the parterre to an elegant gate. In one, a runlet carries water down the long avenue to a large circular fountain. In the other,

which the owners refer to as the jungle walk, the areca palms are planted densely with bamboo, ferns, begonia, orchids, and lilies. In contrast to the bubbling and splashing of the other allée, the jungle walk has its own muffled quality, hidden away from the world and filled with bright wonders.

Near the Meisters' garden, in another part of Palm Beach, a family from Canada commissioned landscape architect Mario Nievera to create a formal garden where they can enjoy the warmth and sunshine. Jonathan Deitcher and his wife, Dianne, had often admired the property on their previous visits to the island. It was an undeveloped lot but boasted beautiful rubber trees and flowering tropical plants. They envisioned a large house where they and their five children could enjoy vacations and a small garden with a pool. But the more they thought about the reality of their schedules, they realized that they rarely traveled with all five children (three are older) and that Mrs. Deitcher's mother's house nearby could accommodate any overflow. And the more they looked at Nievera's plans and the wonderful garden he had designed, their wishes for a large house changed to a desire for a big garden surrounding a house that was just big enough.

Working with Nievera, the Deitchers created a series of outdoor rooms laid out around a seventy-five-foot-long lap pool. Jonathan Deitcher swims for exercise, so the pool was

Opposite: Peninsulas planted with podocarpus transform a long lap pool into an integrated water feature in a Palm Beach garden.
Right: Antique statuary graces a historic Nashville garden designed by the great landscape designer Bryant Fleming in the 1920s and 1930s.

important to the overall scheme. But Nievera recognized the potential hazard of the pool dominating the design, so he gave it the required space but set outcroppings of plantings at intervals down its length to soften its effect. "It looks more like a water element in the garden," says Jonathan. The planted outcroppings form the framework for a series of petite garden rooms, which as you walk down the length of the pool open themselves with pretty vignettes of statuary and urns. "You have the experience of passing through rooms, turning this way and that, catching glimpses of something new with each step," says Nievera.

Nievera also used tall shrubbery, the sixteen-foot-tall podocarpus, to add a strong vertical element to the mix. In shape at least, the podocarpus shrubs have the effect of Italy's cypress trees, with the small, neat leaves so at home in Palm Beach. The strong horizontal axes of pool and lawn are punctuated with the tall hedges and towering rubber trees, their sinewy trunks and limbs reaching to the sky. Around the garden, classic tropical plants provide splashes of color. Pink hibiscus, the Lily Pulitzer of the flower world, seems to require nothing less than bottled water. The graceful statues of the Four Seasons pose like cocktail party guests against the hedges. The house, with two bedrooms, is actually a pool house awaiting the primary house to be built in the future. But with its tidy scale, intimate

relationship to the garden, and expansive privacy, it suits the family nearly too well. That big house may never get built.

Although swimming pools may be de rigueur in Palm Beach, water is in fact an essential element in formal southern gardens. In any civilization that experiences the extreme heat of the American South, water, in the form of fountains and pools, becomes nearly a matter of necessity. Evolving from early irrigation systems in ancient civilizations, the decorative use of water in the garden was born when the function of the garden changed from purely agricultural to one of aesthetic pleasure. In the ancient gardens of Mogul India and Persia, which were strictly formal in design, springs from the mountains were channeled into canals, which then slid down terraced slopes in cascades called *chadars*. Today one of the great

Above: On a Columbus, Georgia, estate, a broad grassy path leads the visitor down a gentle slope from the house to the rondel, a circle garden. **Opposite:** The rondel is punctuated with an oversize urn and ringed with pansies.

American *chadars* exists at Longe Vue plantation and garden in New Orleans. There, in the
worst heat of summer, water flows out of a slot
in the wall and runs down a gently sloped brick
wall, cooling and stirring the air around it. In
the romantic courtyard gardens of Charleston,
fountains burble cheerfully, cooling the air and
masking city noises.

In Texas, where the summer heat drives
some of the citizenry to their mountain refuges
in Aspen, the rest keep cool by swimming.
There, garden design benefits from the influence of neighboring Mexico. In Dallas, pools
are often rimmed in colorful tile and feature
the crafts of Mexican artists. In Austin, with its
abundant hillside sites overlooking Lake Austin,
residents favor infinity swimming pools, with
their illusory invisible edge over which the
pool's water seems to spill into nothingness. The

gardens around these lively water elements
tend to reflect a formal arrangement but are
composed of native plant materials, like
Mexican sage and the ornamental grasses that
thrive in the arid environment.

One of the aspects of a garden that
southerners especially love is well-mannered
profusion. Our heart thrills to the sight of a
'Cécile Brunner' rose bent under the weight
of its boisterous bloom. But some of us also
crave the order and symmetry of formal beds
and pathways. Sally Foley in Columbus,
Georgia, and garden designer P. Allen Smith
laid out a formal garden plan in south
Georgia, and then planted it in a loose,
profuse style more akin to a cottage garden.
The effect is dual: one of instant age, as if all
the towering mature plants had been there
far longer than their ten years, and also one

Advice on Companion Planting from Billy Angell, owner, Oak Street Garden Shop, Birmingham, Alabama:

- One favorite pair for companion planting is dogwood and oakleaf hydrangea. I'm partial to these because they are native plants, and do especially well in a partial shade area. I like a layered look. With its early spring blooms, dogwood makes a perfect understory to tall trees. Hydrangea provides an understory to the dogwood.

- I also like vegetable and herb cultivation, incorporating them into the landscape. Most people don't think of mixing vegetables and herbs with other plantings. They make terrific additions to gardens.

- Things to keep in mind for the southern garden are obviously the heat and lack of cold winters. You must be specific with your choices of plants, which varies depending on which zone you garden in. The whole South encompasses five climate zones. In Birmingham, for example, I recommend tender plants, like gardenias, and mountainous plants such as hemlock, native azaleas, and mountain laurel.

of layering, as the structure recedes and plantings emerge.

A series of terraces solved the problem of breaking up the long slope of property. In many of the South's hilly cities, terraces serve to flatten the land and allow for gardening on otherwise inaccessible hillsides. They also provide boundaries between areas of the garden, allowing you to align outdoor "rooms" without the use of hedges.

Sally Foley loves arranging flowers, and one of her requirements was that the garden produce enough to satisfy her artistic leanings. So there are twenty-six varieties of roses, climbing arches, weaving along fences, and blooming in profusion. The effect of all this frilly excess somewhat softens the sharp edges of the formal garden, proving that in the hands of a skilled and passionate gardener, the formal

garden can be as personal as one desires.

Surely there is no single garden more expressive of a man's focused passion than George Weymouth's hollyhock "room" in the Brandywine River Valley of Delaware. Around a fifty-by-seventy-foot rectangle of lawn inspired by Istanbul's Blue Mosque, Weymouth planted hundreds of old-fashioned hollyhocks, which from June to October bloom in walls of vibrant color. The simplicity of the scheme belies the discipline required to limit yourself to a single flower. Of course, the hollyhock garden does possess a few other plant elements. Landscape architect François Goffinet trained twelve hornbeams into a squared-off arch that frames a sculpture. The eight-to-ten-foot-tall hollyhocks are underplanted to hide the bare stalks near the

Opposite: Long, deep borders lead toward the house in Donna Hackman's Virginia garden.

ground. It is a colorful, natural equivalent to minimalist interior decorating, devoting so much space to a bold statement. And with typically southern aplomb, Weymouth hosts a spontaneous annual tea in his hollyhock garden when the blooms are at their peak. Since it's hard to predict exactly when the flowers will reach perfection, regular guests know to expect very short notice for the invitation to celebrate Weymouth's singular achievement.

One of the great characteristics of southern formal gardens is their charming informality. Whereas the European model of a parterre, with its neatly clipped boxwood laid out in precise patterns, can possess the off-putting air of a regal monarch, the southern version is entirely more approachable. Often, the evergreen box is clipped less severely so that the profile is softer. It is frequently interplanted with material of a more blowzy nature, like buddleia, which lends a free-spirited air to the parterre. Virginia landscape designer Phillip Watson specializes in fresh southern pattern gardens, which he doesn't even pretend to call parterres. He lays out box in grids or plants swirls of impatiens in a rainbow of colors. In one garden he designed for a family that raises horses, Watson created a horseshoe hedge filled with bright tulips. A great sense of fun comes through in Watson's designs, epitomizing the southern approach to formal gardening.

In Virginia, garden designer Donna Hack-

man created a spectacular formal garden for herself that perfectly expresses her own personality. Having never lived in a house long enough to see her garden designs mature, she was determined to see this one through and began planting before she and her family had even moved into the house. Now, eleven years and three acres later, Hackman not only has seen her garden in its full glory but has also developed into a formidable plantswoman. Working with a network of growers from the East Coast to the Pacific Northwest, she has introduced unusual and rare plants into her Virginia estate.

Donna Hackman's large Federal-style house lends itself to the formal garden rooms that surround the brick building. In those long, broad areas, Hackman indulges her passion for color schemes more akin to English perennial borders than flat French parterres. She pairs vibrant pink roses with electric blues of salvia and allium for breathtaking color effects. There are more than sixty roses, which she uses in broad strokes, mixed into plantings of annuals and perennials and allowed to spill over the tops of beds, giving her borders a colorful exuberance. She's retained the majestic white oak trees in her garden to lend a generous dose of Virginia woodland spirit to the space. Strong axes punctuated by planted urns, again brimming with flowers that Hackman changes from year to year depending on current discoveries, accent the formal arrangement with

Opposite: In a woodland garden in Birmingham, Alabama, a formal lawn bordered by perennials to the east of the house catches the afternoon sun. Urns form focal points at either end of the lawn. **Right:** An intimate terrace provides a peaceful spot for contemplation.

typical southern exuberance. Around one neo-classical urn, Hackman planted a wide band of *Cerastium tomentosa*, delicately white-flowered, low-growing, and spreading plants. In nature's serendipity, red snapdragon volunteers sprang up in the urn's shadow, providing an unbridled bull's-eye of color.

Hackman is partial to parterres and has created two areas where she can explore patterns. In one, a more strictly defined garden room, dwarf Alberta spruce trees anchor the four corners of the parterre and add elevation. Pea gravel paths divide the four beds, edged with slate and filled with lavender and edging box. In the other area, situated under the living-room window, where it provides a compelling view, Hackman has established a pair of medieval knot gardens,

drawing her designs using evergreen shrubs in contrasting colors of deep green, icy pale green, and red barberry, which keep the garden interesting in winter.

While southerners will always have an affinity for the tradition of formal gardens, they strive to reinvent the restrained classical model in their own terms. Most want the bones of a formal garden, with the spirit of an English herbaceous border, colorful and gay. The strong visual axis, leading the eye onward through an orderly garden space toward an inspiring focal point, endures as a powerful way to organize a large garden. With its echoes of great gardens of the past, the formal garden appeals to our sense of history. The formal garden in the South is the natural expression of present grandeur and a dazzling future.

COTTAGE GARDENS

Southerners will always love the prolific and complex look of a cottage garden, even if it is applied over a formal framework. The look of roses mingled with phlox, daisies, and salvia, each contributing its delicacy and fragrance to a glorious harmony, has challenged many southern gardeners to nurture plants that have difficulty adapting to our fickle climate. The cottage garden in the South expresses the best of the southern

Opposite: An urn filled with *Sedum acre* gets an unexpected burst of color from an aster planted nearby. **Above:** Snapdragons, 'Indian Summer' rudbeckia, and ageratum make for a festive combination in the Cones' North Carolina cottage garden.

character. It is a place that is intimate, excessive, private, and hospitable. Traditionally, a cottage garden is a small space enclosed by a fence, densely planted with a profusion of flowers, herbs, and vegetables all the way to and sometimes surrounding the door of the house. The house itself dictates the style of cottage garden. Obviously, a grand house in a classical manner, with columns and a Palladian window, does not justify the cottage style garden. Rather, the low-profile, unpretentious country house style of architecture suits the more casual type of garden.

In the modern South, true cottage gardens are rare. It is rather the cottage influence you see more often, in seemingly casual plant arrangements; mixed plantings of annuals, perennials, herbs, and vegetables; and dense planting plans. In fact, authentic cottage gardens, like the ones we imagine formed the topography of Beatrix Potter books, may be as fictional as Peter Rabbit. As British garden writer Christopher Llyod wrote in *The Cottage Garden:* "Although appearing free and easy, the best kind of cottage garden is actually well organized, otherwise nature would take over, and nature is no gardener."

The life of an English peasant, in which the cottage style theoretically originated, was not conducive to the pretty, flower-filled garden that we think of today. Meat played a primary role in the diet of the cottager and was given priority in the limited confines of the cottage yard, which was more likely to be a simple patch for growing a few vegetables and keeping a pig and chickens, and perhaps a beehive. Flowers and decorative plantings would do little to feed a family. In fact, cottage gardens as we know them flourished during the period of prosperity in the late eighteenth century as the gentry moved out of the city to the country villages in search of a simplified, pastoral quality of life. There, with the leisure to tend and maintain a garden, and the financial security to support a garden purely for pleasure, the new country gentry, in fact "city folk," invented the cottage garden.

Opposite: In Donna Hackman's Middleburg, Virginia, garden, a pristine wooden fence creates an inviting entryway into an area of the cottage garden. **Above:** Formal gardens near the house give way to a spacious cottage garden down a sloping hillside.

Opposite and right: Dense plantings, broken by artfully arranged stones and a cascading rivulet, create a fairy-tale atmosphere in Hackman's Virginia wonderland.

Gertrude Jekyll, the renowned landscape designer, popularized the cottage style during the Victorian era. Like William Robinson before her, Jekyll took elements from historic cottage gardens and applied them to commissions in England and France. With an emphasis on native plants, no matter how humble, Jekyll promoted a garden style that was more natural than the previous formal style, and more in harmony with the English countryside. Jekyll's influence spilled down through succeeding generations of gardeners, particularly Vita Sackville-West, whose garden at Sissinghurst has captivated many southern gardeners looking to England for inspiration.

Bursting with lupines, primroses, and pinks, as well as herbs and vegetables, the garden usually was situated in front of the house, divided down the middle by a path running to the front door. On either side of the path, beds of mingled flowering plants bloomed with such profusion that they spilled over onto the pathways. In fact, the experience of pushing your way through the lush planting to reach the front door was essential to enjoying the cottage garden. Your motion would set the flowers dancing. The birds and butterflies would take flight. Your touch would likely release the fragrance of the flowers and herbs.

Although a cottage garden may appear at first glance to be a profusion of random plantings, it, like all gardens, requires thoughtful planning. The beds must be laid so that weeding and tending can take place without crushing other plants. Often a cottage gardener will employ a formal garden outline but then blur the edges with a more casual approach to planting. A parterre can accommodate varied, colorful plantings and convey the coveted cottage appearance. Plants may be placed close together for a full and lush look, but they need proper nutrients to thrive. You see the cottage influence in the meandering woodland gardens of Virginia, in a rose garden embraced by split-rail fences, and in the riotously planted pots in a Charleston courtyard. Wherever the garden teeters on the brink of disorder, wherever the serendipity of nature is allowed expression, the cottage garden spirit is present.

When Jekyll introduced the seemingly unkempt look to a startled public, she said, "I hold the heresy of not minding a little moss on the paths and of rather preferring a few scattered clusters of rose petals on its brown-green velvet." She continued that there was nothing at all

Left: A crape myrtle provides a colorful backdrop for an exciting display of varying textures.
Opposite: Scattered rose petals on the lush turf convey a deliberately unkempt look.

careless about the cottage style: "In the way it is done," she said, "lies the whole difference between commonplace gardening and gardening that very rightly claims to rank as fine art." With her painter's eye and appreciation for texture (she was actually extremely nearsighted) Jekyll created gardens that were masterful combinations of color and form.

One quality that everyone associates with cottage gardens is a feeling of enclosure. That sense may be created by walls, hedges, tall trees, or simply plantings of tall plants. Allen Lacy writes, in *The Inviting Garden:* "The gardens I like best share some things. First, they are enclosed, and second, they are inviting — in part because they are enclosed." He goes on to cite the courtyard gardens of Charleston as the epitome of the inviting garden, and no doubt Emily Whaley would have agreed. "Virtually none is

open to the street. At most, the passing stranger can catch only a glimpse of what lies behind their high walls of brick or their ornate wrought iron fences, although some plants spill over into public spaces." While the typical Charleston garden is not strictly a cottage garden, it does share with that tradition a diminutive aspect, abundant but careful planting, and a proximity to the house. Herbs play an important role in the cottage garden. They may have constituted the very earliest precursors to cottage gardens, little beds of herbs grown close to the house. They were grown not only for culinary uses but also for the medicinal values and for their scent, which masked a multitude of odors, from household mildew to bad breath. Popular cottage herbs include mint, marjoram, parsley, rosemary, dill, and lavender. Southerners like herbs as much for their appearance as for their usefulness. From the

Opposite: The essential accessory of any cottage garden—a portly, hospitable dog. **Right:** The gardener borders her loosely planted parterre with a fence from which every other board has been omitted, permitting a view beyond the garden.

fine feathers of fennel to the glossy broad leaves of basil, herbs can fill in bare patches and provide valuable companion plantings. In the South, rosemary thrives in the ground, performing better than its counterparts contained in pots. One Birmingham landscape designer, Mary Zahl, likes to intersperse parsley among her perennials. Its bright green, compact growth habit makes it a good companion plant for large-leafed and silvery plants. In the mild climate, it stays green all winter, providing life when everything else has gone dormant for the season.

There are many annuals that survive the southern winter to sprout again in the spring, which are referred to alternately as hardy annuals or tender perennials. The exceptional behavior of many plants in the southern climate renders many garden guides, especially those written about English gardens or gardens of the American Northeast, incorrect or misleading for southern readers. Therefore, it has been especially important for southerners to create their own version of the English cottage garden, since many of the staples of that plan, like hybrid lupines, just do not perform as well here, depending as they do on wet autumns and winters.

Instead, southern cottage gardeners make the most of the plants that thrive here, like rudbeckia, cosmos, and hydrangeas. Foxgloves provide that vertical bolt of color that lupines do in the English garden. The mingling of very different types of plants — roses with vegetables,

for instance — is another characteristic of the traditional cottage garden and one that has taken its time catching on in the southern scheme.

Intrepid southern gardeners are discovering the joyful and surprising combinations that are possible with the more disease-resistant old-fashioned and antique roses. Growers like Mike Shoup, of Texas's Antique Rose Emporium, have made it their crusade to repopularize these historic and prolific bloomers. With nearly no maintenance required, they blend in happily with plantings of all sorts.

One gardener outside Baltimore has successfully blended a vegetable garden and a flower garden behind her house. On the rather large property, Suzy Russell carved out a fifty-foot square and planted it thickly with daisies, lettuces, foxgloves, and peas. Her garden is arranged in a rough parterre, but within that formal framework the planting is anything but rigid. She fills in any bare spot with plants chosen for color or texture, her aim being to create a blanket of vivid, mixed colors. Though she began the garden with more vegetables than flowers, the ratio has gradually reversed as her children grew up and moved away, and the demands for edibles from the garden diminished.

Previous pages: In Liz Clooney's garden in a historic neighborhood in Birmingham, Alabama, lush plantings of hosta, astilbe, and oakleaf hydrangea create a magical mix of color and texture. A stone walkway cuts a subtle path through the plantings. **Above:** Gigantic, mature oakleaf hydrangeas create a secret-garden entry to Clooney's garden. **Opposite:** Cosmos, delphinium, peonies, and roses frame a cottagelike entry to Sally and Alan Cone's house in Greensboro.

Russell's approach is typical of most southern gardeners craving the boisterous look of a cottage garden on a sizable piece of property. One couldn't realistically fill it edge to edge with plantings. Having created a self-contained cottage garden set away from the house, Russell finds herself spending much of the warm weather outdoors rather than in the house. Like many others, Russell relies on the thoughtfulness of friends who know to seek her out among her beloved plants when she's unreachable by phone. At Devonshire, a great garden shop in Palm Beach, they sell a front-door sign that seems designed for the southern gardener. On a simple painted board, the words I'M IN THE GARDEN send the region's summer sentiment.

Another gardener in Birmingham, Alabama, started her cottage garden near the house but over the years has gradually let her plantings spread to the property's edge. Linda Johnson has a passion for gardening, probably inherited from her mother and father, both of whom tended gardens all their lives. In fact, Johnson has a rosebush that she got from her mother, who got it from *her* mother, so the gardening inheritance is quite literally represented in that one cherished plant. On antiquing trips to the Cotswolds, Johnson became enamored of the profuse and overgrown look of the cottage gardens there. So in her own Eden she planted roses, hollyhocks, and Queen Anne's lace to capture the romantic

feeling. She often leaves the front door open, inviting in the heady scents of roses and herbs and enhancing the feeling of being nestled in a mature garden. When leaves, pollen, and the occasional lost chipmunk stray in, Johnson remains sanguine. A little mess is a small price to pay for living in a garden's embrace.

In Johnson's garden, the furniture and ornamentation stay true to the cottage tradition. Worn garden benches, a rustic archway, and antique urns seem to rise out of the growth like organic elements. Weathered ornaments, peeling paint, and everyday objects (like watering cans) used as accents characterize the cottage garden. A rustic archway frames a view of the trees and threatens to be consumed by a ballerina rose. Wrens nest in a birdhouse made of bark, with a little peaked

Opposite: Becky Thompson has an intimate relationship with her Little Rock, Arkansas, cottage-style garden. A path sweeps by a border of 'Mary Webb' roses.
Right: Landscape architect Chip Calloway designed a Greensboro, North Carolina, garden that perfectly blends the bones of a formal parterre with fanciful cottage plantings, including jaunty rose standards.

roof. A plain wooden bench invites loitering among the flowers and birds. Palatial fountains crowned with majestic mythological figures belong to the formal gardening tradition. Unobtrusive, utilitarian features blend in to the cottage garden, not so much grabbing attention as contributing to the tapestry of color and texture.

One of the distinguishing characteristics of cottage gardens is the style of architectural elements used for boundaries and accents. Gates, which can provide such an important moment of entry from the street, are modest and informal. Hedges form the classic cottage-garden boundary, whether composed of holly, hawthorn, privet, or pyracantha. Although they don't need to be as perfectly pruned as the shrubbery in a formal garden, they do need to be trimmed a couple of times a year. As a

natural boundary, hedges have the disadvantage of being extremely slow to establish. For that reason, many cottage gardeners prefer to build a low stone wall or a fence. Rather than ornate ironwork, fences, like gates, tend to be made of rough-hewn branches or boards, or crisp white pickets. At Seaside, Florida, with its supremely cottagey atmosphere, all the houses are required to have picket fences, and no two picket patterns can be alike! There, the cottage garden feeling is achieved with native plants interspersed with tough perennials like rudbeckia.

Pathways in cottage gardens tend to wander more than formal garden paths. Southerners love to use local stone slabs for a loose pathway that gives the garden an organic feeling. There are few sharp turns, and no right angles. Instead, a path meanders through the plantings, allowing you to enjoy

Left: In Blowing Rock, North Carolina, a rustic log fence provides the perfect cottage garden boundary. Below: Blueberries mix with flowers in this classic cottage garden. Opposite: In their Blowing Rock garden, the Cones erected a little cedar-roofed pergola to relate the garden to the cottage on the hillside above.

the blooms, permitting you a voyage of discovery. Stones set into the beds allow access for weeding without disrupting the planting. Brick paths tend to be made of loosely laid salvaged bricks with rounded edges. Though they look charming, brick paths can present a safety hazard if the bricks get too uneven or if moss is allowed to spread. Gravel paths are a perfect solution, adding the satisfying crunch underfoot to the sensory experience of the garden.

In a magical garden nestled in a mountainside in Blowing Rock, North Carolina, pathways of thick green grass divide the beds. Although the garden itself is set a short distance from the house, the owner, Janet Cone, placed a little cottage in its midst to be used as a toolshed. The plants crowd around the toolshed in an affectionate imitation of a classic cottage garden. Filled with foxgloves, 'Indian Summer' rudbeckia, snapdragons, blueberries, Oriental lilies, and white pompom dahlias, the Cone garden speaks fluent cottage vernacular.

With its climate so similar to the English one — cool summers and low humidity — Blowing Rock is ideally suited to cottage gardening. The style of architecture of south-

ern mountain homes, usually a cabin or bungalow, encourages the profuse, flowery style. At the Cones', the colors seem to sparkle in the clear air — crisp white, blazing pink, and glowing blue. Towering fir trees surround the garden, enclosing it and filtering the sunlight. In this secure embrace, the garden has a fairy-tale quality, like an enchanted garden stumbled upon by accident.

The drama in a cottage garden does not lie in the vistas or a single focal point; it depends instead on the quiet intimacy experienced with color and fragrance, sound and texture. There are certainly visual treats, such as statuary tucked into a surprising nook. You might round a corner to find a delightful little fountain or

birdbath. Although a narrow pathway is more in keeping with cottage tradition, it impedes companionable walks through the garden when a friend comes to visit and you want to stroll side by side, discussing plants. For that reason, most gardeners make pathways wide enough for two people to walk abreast.

Water is another comfortable companion in a southern cottage garden. Whereas a formal garden might feature an imposing,

classically inspired fountain, a cottage garden calls for a more modest approach. Gardeners who live on a sloping site might dig a narrow channel, skirting rocks and other obstacles, to provide a sylvan splash of water. A little waterfall adds fairy-tale romance to a garden, as does a diminutive fountain edged with stones. Ponds can be carved out of the soil and planted with lush water plants, the edges blurred by water-loving growth. Originally

Below: An antique glass cloche protects seedlings in a bed of *Salvia leucantha.*
Opposite: A mock orange, 'Natchez' sheds its petals after a hard rain. In Little Rock, Arkansas, Becky Thompson doesn't deadhead, preferring instead to follow the bloom through its full cycle of life.

used by cottagers as a home for ducks and geese, ponds have become a decorative luxury, and one that can lull the visitor into contemplative reverie.

A gardener in Little Rock, Arkansas, scours flea markets for antique architectural pieces to place around her garden. A garden designer by trade, Becky Thompson favors old cupolas and tucks them down in grassy meadows so their jaunty spires seem to salute from the garden. Like Linda Johnson in Birmingham, Thompson enjoys spending time in her garden and

has even built a little teahouse where she and her granddaughter can hide out and read. One of the primary diffferences between a formal garden and a cottage garden is that the former is designed primarily for the eye. It is meant to be seen, with its powerful axis drawing the eye onward, and its patterns are best appreciated from afar. But a cottage garden is meant to be experienced on more levels. It is a string quartet as opposed to the formal garden's symphony orchestra. It is meant to be wandered through, touched, inhaled, even tasted. With its smaller scale, the drama of a cottage garden is domestic, allowing an immediate and intimate relationship. The play of light on a leaf or the progress of a bumblebee makes up the tragedy and triumph of a morning in the cottage garden.

Thompson studies her garden closely, watching as the roses change from day to day, noting each new bloom over her morning coffee. She keeps a garden diary, charting the life of the garden, which is inextricably entwined with her own. Every morning she notes the aspect of each plant, the disposition of the roses, the waning of the geraniums. With a gardening philosophy rooted in cottage principles, she never deadheads her flowers, cherishing the fading of the bloom as much as its opening.

Although Thompson's garden is bigger than the peasant cottager's of old, like many other

CHAPTER 2: COTTAGE GARDENS

Opposite: Roses are most at home in a cottage garden. **Following pages:** On Robert Hill and Anthony Fant's terrace in Birmingham, a cottage feel is established with pots and planters filled with blooming flowers.

From Mike Shoup of the Antique Rose Emporium, Brenham, Texas

Best Roses for the South:

Tea roses: originally from China, have adapted themselves to the South, truly southern ("grandmother's roses"), fragrant, pastel. Examples: 'Mrs. B. R. Cant' (big, voluptuous, spreads to five feet by five feet, big silvery pink flowers, fragrant); 'Duchess de Brabant'; 'Maman Cochet'; 'Safrano'; 'Mrs. Dudley Cross' (yellow, thornless); 'Monsieur Tillier' (red)

China roses: similar to tea roses, from China, heat-tolerant, like teas but flowers less full, useful as hedges, in containers, to create lines. Examples: 'Old Blush' (pink, everblooming thick, chunky shrub, "can't beat it," also comes in climbing form); 'Archduke Charles' (red and white); 'Mutabilis' (multicolors, begins yellow, then orange-red, then red); 'Louis Philippe' (red)

Noisettes: graceful, climbing, everblooming, flowers hang down like bells, romantic. Notable examples: 'Lamarque,' 'Céline Forestier,' 'Mme. Alfred Carrière,' 'Reve d'Or'

Polyanthid class (small roses): to create mass or for containers, not true "old garden" (about 1900)

"Treat old roses with no special attention. Use them as part of the overall landscape. In pruning and tending, keep them appropriate in scale and size to others around them. Embellish the fact that they are true garden plants, therefore putting less pressure on the gardener — the garden looks great whether the roses are blooming or not. Ignore strict rules about the isolation of roses, and fit them to the scale of the garden."

cooperative blooming habit are an essential part of the mix. 'Heritage,' a David Austin rose, with dense pink blooms and glossy green leaves, makes a classic statement. A rose-laden arbor is almost a signature of a southern garden. Vigorous climbers like 'New Dawn' grow up pergolas, bridge archways, climb into tree branches, and even mount rooftops around the South. Along with clematis, another popular climber, roses suit the southern penchant for dramatic bursts of color. With their constant state of change, from buds to blossoms and falling petals, they provide an enchanting ongoing drama for the gardener.

Tea roses will always have a place in the southern garden, providing so much material for arrangements inside the house. As gardeners grow more sophisticated about mixing roses in with other flowers, vegetables, and herbs, the tea rose threatens to be left out of the mix. Its need for frequent applications of special fertilizers, pesticides, and fungicides makes it a dangerous neighbor for produce intended for eating. Antique roses, on the other hand, don't behave in such histrionic fashion when confronted by disease. With their sturdier disposition, antiques can flourish in the midst of varied plantings. Their graceful, arching branches and plentiful, if smaller, blossoms mean that antique roses maximize the space you give them. Also, the more subdued hues of antique roses have the soft charm necessary for a classic cottage garden.

southern gardeners desiring the enclosed space of a cottage garden, she carved hers into rooms. By dividing up the property into manageable portions, the gardener can create the sense of intimacy and enclosure that a cottage garden requires. She has also created a miniature version of the English countryside. The rooms of perennials, banks of roses, and sculpture are arranged near the house, and beyond a row of hemlock trees, her woodland and wildflower meadows exend into the wilderness.

Roses are especially at home in the cottage garden. The old-fashioned variety, with their sweet, showy blooms, delicious scent, and

Opposite: An outgrown playhouse, complete with cedar shingles and robin's-egg-blue shutters, creates an old-fashioned focal point in this Maryland garden. **Right:** A rosarian in Maryland constructed her garden to make the most of an impressive collection of rose specimens. 'New Dawn,' 'Eden,' and lamb's ears soften the pergola.

Nursery owners are continually exhorting their customers to mix up their plantings. But southerners, with their love of tea roses, have been stubborn in their commitment to the formal rose garden, with the roses isolated from other plantings. The hybrid tea rose's need for constant protection from pests and disease has dictated this sort of planting, to keep the roses a safe distance from one another, lest disease jump from one rose to the next, and also to concentrate the efforts of fungicides and pesticides.

With a fourteen-acre estate to fill with her gardening fancies, a Maryland gardener has created one of the prettiest rose gardens around, in addition to several other charming scenes. What started as a project to simply clear underbrush from the dogwoods has evolved over the years into a sprawling garden of connected rooms. In the rose garden, 'Eden' joins the 'New Dawn' on a pergola, the two roses mingling their pale pink hues. A maritime rope braided with roses and underplanted with peonies guards one edge of the garden. Surrounding the roses, a simple fence of split rails and wire encloses planted beds. Elsewhere, the gardener trained a climbing rose to the roofline of a playhouse her children had outgrown. Its cedar shingles and diminutive size create a cottage scene of incomparable sweetness. On her large property, the gardener has created a progression of intimate gardens, each with its own surprise. Paths connecting the gardens

urge the visitor onward to the next discovery.

Other plants that work well for the cottage garden include lamb's ears, with its laughably apt name and soft, furry leaves. Its generous growing habit and ability to spread make it the perfect plant to fill in blank spaces. Lavender is an English classic, for its scent and for its spires of pale purple flowers that spill like mist over a garden path; however, it does not flourish in humid heat. Sunflowers, with their forthright demeanor and large flower, add height. Purple coneflower, with its old-fashioned, daisylike bloom, is another welcome addition. Buddleia lives up to its common name, butterfly bush, by attracting colorful butterflies and bees all summer long. Sweet peas, snapdragons, stock, and nasturtiums all do well in the southern cottage garden, although a rainless, hot summer can reduce their proliferative blooming.

Lack of rain and intense heat are the southern cottage gardener's age-old nemeses. Somehow, though, each spring, when the memory of the previous season's frustrations

Opposite: Parterres of boxwood, fancifully pruned and punctuated with vertical firs, typify Atlanta landscape architect Ryan Gainey's confident, knowledgeable hand.

has dimmed, and tantalizing images from garden catalogs arrive in the mailbox, gardeners are seized with optimism for the coming summer. The reemergence of perennials from the warming soil seems to encourage this fantasy. The wisteria blooming in showy abandon further loosens their grip on reason. They sharpen their pruning shears, start seeds in peat cups, write vast checks to the garden center, and set about realizing their dream. They would do well to summon a landscaping company to install an irrigation system, but in their impatience to get their Eden under way, they vow to make do with hoses. And indeed, many lush southern gardens are maintained by diligent gardeners with sprinklers and hoses. But come August, there's not a gardening soul in the South who doesn't wish with all his might for an irrigation system lying snugly underground.

Garden experts around the South have encouraged smart watering, but the idea is so counterintuitive that is has been slow to catch on. The theory is that if you water deeply but less frequently early in the season, the plants are encouraged to grow deeper and stronger roots, thereby preparing them to take care of themselves later in the season. A plant with long, strong roots can survive a dry spell better than its lush but essentially weak counterpart. Recent droughts, with water restrictions in some areas, have impressed upon gardeners the

surprising resilience of many plants. Some that were expected to wilt and die without daily watering did wilt but revived nicely when the restrictions were lifted. They are probably stronger for the experience, too, like humans growing stronger through adversity.

For southern gardeners, there are as many possibilities as there are challenges. Each summer of their life teaches them lessons, which hopefully they can study during the dormant winter months. When spring comes, and magazines like *Southern Accents* present examples of vibrant lush cottage gardens, optimism will prevail. Hopefully, the experience of the previous year has equipped them to refine their approach: watering less, spacing farther apart, recognizing their own limitations. The perfect garden may be the one we achieve through balance. When we judiciously exert our own influence, and recognize what nature can do better, both the garden and the gardener will survive the summer.

The cottage garden, with its varied plantings and complicated arrangements of color and texture, relies heavily on the gardener's judgment. When plants coexist so closely together, they need to complement one another not only in hue and growing habit but also in their blooming seasons. But when the gardener gets the right mix, and the right balance, there is nothing more charming in the world than a proper cottage garden.

CHAPTER THREE

LAWNS, HEDGES, AND TREES

*W*hile colorful beds of flowers, artfully arranged for maximum impact, consume much of the gardener's interest and provide proud moments at the height of bloom, the bones of a garden are the trees, shrubs, and lawns. A special tree — like the white oak in Donna Hackman's Middleburg, Virginia, garden, which sprouted long before she ever saw the property and probably long before she was born — can give a formal garden an established quality. A sophisticated plantswoman, Hackman

Opposite: In this Nashville garden designed by Ben Page, a broad grassy path leads enticingly over a hill. **Above:** The dense hedges at historic Glen Burnie in Winchester, Virginia, serve as a theatrical backdrop for the classical statuary.

79

appreciates her oak's character and maturity as much as she enjoys the rare flowering plants she hunts down from growers around the country.

In these days of peripatetic family life, moving frequently to bigger and better quarters is common. The cost can be high, not only in terms of shattered heirlooms and mover's bills. For a gardener, the big payoffs require years of patience, waiting for shrubs to establish and trees to mature. No wonder so few of us are willing to make the long-term landscaping investments, when it is likely we'll never see the results. Donna Hackman had suffered through several moves, leaving behind adolescent gardens, before moving into her Middleburg house. When she and her husband bought the property, Hackman began planting before they even moved in,

hoping to win herself a season's head start. Eleven years later, having finally stayed in one house for an extended period of time, she has realized her dream and has expanded her efforts over three acres of the property.

A majestic tree, whether a live oak, a magnolia, or a tropical banyan tree, can lend a garden a precise sense of place and should give the gardener a starting point for other plantings. Unless absolutely necessary, a mature tree should be spared when clearing land. Gardeners like Ben Page, who charted the passages of his life by the height of the sugar maple his grandfather planted to celebrate Ben's birth, consider such trees essential to a family's history. Southerners have a deep-rooted attachment not only to the land but also to its

distinctive features, like the trees, creeks, and hillsides that give it character.

A long expanse of lawn is a classic element of the southern garden. Its simple, bold form is soothing to the human spirit, and its cool, even surface is a balm to the senses. It provides that peaceful margin between the house and the street, a buffer zone between the private world and the public arena. In the sense that a garden holds back the wilderness, a lawn simply defies disorder. It is nature fully tamed, flourishing under the care of mankind. Underfoot, the tickle of uniform blades of grass takes you back to childhood, when the world extended not much farther than the edge of that lawn. For many southerners, that carefully tended oblong or rectangle spread out like an apron on the domestic homefront is as much a part of the house as the plumbing.

Emily Whaley said in her charming account of a gardening life, *Mrs. Whaley and Her Charleston Garden:* "Grass is a must-have. We want our flower beds overflowing with the colors of the rainbow, but a garden is also a place of repose and order. Grass is the answer. Think about it. Grass is all one color and every leaf is the same shape and cut to the same height. It's smooth and velvety and gives the area a distinctly defined edge. In short, grass is a resting place. . . . Grass is a reprieve for the eye and the mind."

Grass is such a simple element, and yet its impact is complicated. The smell of freshly cut grass, now packaged as room scents and even perfume, has an intense psychological effect. Along with the splash of a sprinkler and the feeling of sunshine on winter-white shoulders, it brings back childhood summer with its attendant excitement and anticipation. Freshly mown lawns cause you to recall long-ago games of tag and leapfrog and gymnastics competitions that left you breathless and scratchy. Joggers in the South know the heady effect of a waft of dewy lawn carried across the warming breeze in the early morning.

As a therapeutic exercise, nothing beats pushing a rotary lawn mower, what one gardener calls his "acoustic" mower, back and forth

across the grass after work. The whir of the blades, the fine shower of grass cuttings, and the satisfaction of neat rows of cut lawn behind you can lift the day's woes like nothing else. The aromatherapy you receive in the process is lagniappe. While most gardeners love to complain about the upkeep lawns require, they likely receive abundant pleasure in the act of tending the grass.

The suburban American lawn was an idea fostered first by Andrew Jackson Downing, whose plea for peaceful stretches of public lawn made possible the vast expanse of New York's Central Park, and then more influentially by Frank Scott. In 1870 Scott published a treatise titled *The Art of Beautifying Suburban Home Grounds of Small Extent*. His idea, that adjoining parcels of suburban property should be linked by expanses of grassy lawns, thus

Grass Seed Recipe from Glen Burnie

- The grass at Glen Burnie historic gardens is so lush and green that visitors continually inquire as to its makeup. The gardeners finally resorted to posting the recipe outside the greenhouse. When couples get married at Glen Burnie, the guests throw handfuls of the seed mixture.

- 29.4% Shenandoah

- 14.7% Winchester

- 14.7% Renegade

- 14.7% Veranda

- 14.7% Falcon II

- 9.7% Debutant

- 2.1% inert matter

Opposite: Bordered by two walls of Hatfield yews, the statue garden of Glen Burnie in Virginia is a peaceful haven. **Below:** At Tyreconnell in Baltimore, Maryland, tall hedges extend a stone wall and lead the visitor to the allée of stone steps up the hillside.

providing a shared public space between each citizen's doorway and the street, led to the classic suburban layout: street, lawn leading up to the door, foundation plantings, and a garden behind the house. Indeed, Scott wrote in strong terms about what he perceived as the near criminal offense of putting up fences: "It is unchristian to hedge from the sight of others the beauties of nature which it has been our good fortune to create or secure, and all of the walls, high fences, hedge screens, and belts of trees and shrubbery which are used for this purpose are only so many means by which we show how unchristian and unneighborly we can be."

The garden writer Allen Lacy takes on Scott, and all lawn lovers, in his book *The Inviting Garden*. He suggests that lawns were born of the new working class's insecurities as they moved to the suburbs and began to

contend with the spaces surrounding their houses. Out of bourgeois fear of revealing low-class origins, early suburban residents at the turn of the century gobbled up books that offered advice on how to make an American home. And Frank Scott, among others, fed that hunger with his pastoral images of family life in the verdant country, with the father traveling into the city by rail each day to provide his family a high quality of life. And part of that high quality of life included a parklike lawn, based on the landscapes of grand estates and imported to the suburbs.

Lacy, a proponent of private garden spaces and a worshiper of Charleston courtyard gardens, would see lawns eliminated as part of the American garden vocabulary: "It would be delightful if everyone in the country would immediately kill the grass in their front yards (or

at least reduce its extent) and rip up half of the shrubs huddled against their house foundations and put them on the periphery of their property. I see nothing but good coming as a result."

Of course, we know that lawns are an impractical American obsession, an aberrant gardening habit. Nothing is less natural than a lawn, or harder to maintain. We've heard it all before. Weeds love to infiltrate the grass, bare spots appear and grow relentlessly despite your frenzied efforts to diagnose and treat the problem. Grass burns in the heat, needs incessant watering, and, of course, mowing. And yet southerners are as likely to give up their lawns as they are to renounce sending thank-you notes. Southern gardeners love challenges. Just tell them that a certain plant cannot grow in their zone and they'll set out to prove you wrong. The

battle to establish and maintain a pretty lawn is one that southerners take on with ferocity. Serious gardeners who take pride in their hands-on efforts sneer at those gardeners with pockets deep enough to fund an underground sprinkler system. Yet, come August, as those without subterranean water sources drag hoses all over their property while their neighbors sit smugly on their porches drinking mint juleps listening to the staccato of the sprinklers — well, let's just say tempers can flare in the heat.

So we stubbornly maintain our gardens, weeding, seeding, and mowing in pursuit of that flawless green vista. Southerners traveling to England have given in to envy of the apparently effortless lush lawns at every turn. As one Englishman reputedly replied when asked how he achieved such even green, "Well, you just

Opposite: A symphony of color and pattern emerges from a Ben Page–designed Nashville garden, with chartreuse barberry, 'Bagatelle' barberry, and boxwood.
Below right: In a Birmingham, Alabama, garden, Mary Zahl fashions woven patterns of evergreen shrubs on both sides of a pathway, creating a foreground for the house.
Below left: An enormous, spiral-carved yew topiary is the centerpiece of the Nashville garden, where Page has created textural interest with a wide variety of hedges.

water it and mow it once a week or so . . . for about four hundred years." A lawn is a dauntingly long-term endeavor, coming into its own when fully mature. A solid root system can keep out weeds and keep the grass drought-resistant. However, many southern gardeners with dreams of green gaze out upon a patchwork of sod, like a sloppily built brick wall.

A lawn on its own is a magnificent sight, but a swath of lawn also serves to highlight other elements of the garden. It can give contrast to a colorful, textured perennial bed.

It can emphasize the shape and stature of a prized tree. It can lead the eye to a surprising focal point. It can be the backdrop to an architectural element near the house. A calm stretch of grass serves as a pause, a prelude to the further exploration of a garden. Like a musical rest, it allows the senses to take a breath before continuing onward. A square or rectangle sets up the rhythm for a formal garden, with symmetry and pairs of plantings, opposing borders, and orderly axes. An oblong or curving area of grass lends itself to casual planting schemes, gradual mixing of plantings, and intimate garden spaces. A grassy path winding through a garden creates anticipation, mystery, and a desire to discover what may lie beyond the bend.

Below: Alexander palms stand like sculpture in an outdoor room in Palm Beach. **Opposite above:** Hedges create a privacy wall behind a Hobe Sound, Florida, swimming pool. **Opposite below:** In Palm Beach, Florida, order prevails, with hedges arching over a wide gated entrance and niches neatly cutting out for urns.

Hedges serve a variety of purposes. They can enclose, enfolding the garden with protective arms. They can arouse curiosity, standing just high enough to allow a tempting peek into an outdoor room. They can invite neighborly chats from yard to yard. They can shut the world out entirely, giving a garden walls of dense green. Nowhere do hedges do more to establish the personality of a place than in Palm Beach, Florida. Like its northern cousins, Southampton and East Hampton, New York, Palm Beach is an exclusive community mostly made up of second homes, where the privileged few go to relax.

There, ficus hedges are clipped and pruned and grown to a paparazzi-blocking height of up to twenty feet. The experience of driving down a residential Palm Beach street is one of thwarted curiosity. The slim opening between the hedges permits only a passing glance of a driveway, with a Bentley or a Jaguar pulled up to a courtyard entrance. The thick branches permit only fractured views of what lies beyond them. A blue sparkle hints at a swimming pool, a burst of laughter suggests an exclusive afternoon tea. How painfully tantalizing to stand just feet away from the party at hand! And how delightful to be a guest, surrounded by the protective walls of green.

Mario Nievera, a Palm Beach landscape designer, is familiar with the habits and function of hedges. At the Deitcher residence in Palm Beach, he created a richly textured garden with hedges and shrubs of varied heights, punctuated with spires of podocarpus. A long swimming pool, inset with outcroppings of planted beds all along its length, has the effect of a more subtle water feature. While the garden shows very little color, it is dramatic nonetheless, with the great swirling trunk of a rubber tree standing majestically flanked by neatly restrained beds of plantings. It also has the look of a more mature garden because of tall shrubs like the podocarpus that Nievera planted throughout the space. All along the length of the pool, Nievera used hedges to create a series of little outdoor rooms framing

Opposite: In a Palm Beach garden by Mario Nievera, along a walkway leading to the gate, the trunk of a palm tree could easily be mistaken for one of the coquina columns. **Right:** In his own garden, Phillip Watson experiments with a palette of greens in a parterre. **Below:** Jorge Sanchez takes advantage of thick-growing hedges to carve doorways, incorporating metal gates to emphasize the architectural reference.

vignettes of garden statuary. The little rooms propel you down the pathway, your attention drawn first right, then left as the statuary catches your eye.

Another Palm Beach landscape architect, Jorge Sanchez, loves the effects he achieves with hedges. "They can be tall and very straight, which gives an impressive effect. I can also think of one that's twenty-five feet tall with a wavy pattern that is quite beautiful," he says. He admits that *Ficus nitida*, also known as Cuban laurel, is the "bread and butter" of Palm Beach hedges. "It offers privacy from the outside world and also allows you to create rooms within the garden. It is a good 'putty' to work with in the garden, because it gives you so much form."

Sanchez is fond of carving doors and

windows through hedges, further suggesting their kinship to walls. He links hedges to gates and walls in a masterful blending of materials. While in Palm Beach an opening may offer no more than a peek of what lies beyond, in other places it can frame a dramatic vista, like a view of mountains or fields. In keeping with the southern character, hedges permit gardeners to hide and reveal exactly what they choose — giving a glimpse of a home or garden, retaining a favored view to private enjoyment.

Another region that takes much of its identity from hedges is the horse country around Middleburg, Virginia. There, the horse pastures and riding trails spread across the rolling landscape like a blanket. The large estates, with their expansive gardens, are separated from the manicured "wild" areas with low hedges, offering both a view of the distance and an opportunity for jumping on horseback.

With their abiding passion for formal gardens, southerners are especially fond of fashioning hedges into parterres, creating geometric patterns in their gardens. Phillip Watson, a Virginia landscape architect, has made parterres a specialty, exploring schemes both

Previous pages: Four different types of boxwoods create a garden of great interest through geometrics. **Above left:** Ben Page planted a hedge of 'Winter King' hawthorn in a Nashville garden. **Above right:** A natural hedge of hawthorn defines a semicircular lawn. **Opposite:** A boxwood hedge lines a walkway and creates a solid edge for the blowsy show of hydrangeas.

grand and amusing in his work. In his own garden, a parterre in shades of dark box and chartreuse astilbe plays an ode to a green palette, bordered by a neat wall of Leyland cypress hedge. In a client's courtyard, Watson planted a grid of neat squares of boxwood for a minimalist statement. For a client who raises thoroughbreds, he created a horseshoe out of boxwood. In a Jackson, Mississippi, garden, he planted a rainbow of impatiens in a sweeping arc that greets you from the front door but is invisible from the street.

One of the great advantages of parterres made primarily of shrubs like boxwood is that they require very little maintenance other than pruning. Interplanting with flowers can provide great shows of color in the spring and summer, and the garden will retain its graphic strength during the cold months when the flowers die

back. Donna Hackman planted her parterres right under a sitting-room window, where she can enjoy their lines from the cozy fireside even when they're cloaked in a blanket of snow. Working with varieties of box and barberry, Hackman has created a painterly parterre of russet, pine green, and chartreuse.

Another gardener in Nashville, Tennessee, worked with landscape architect Ben Page to create a magnificent estate garden that relies heavily on strong shapes of boxwood topiary and hedges. The centerpiece of the garden is a giant boxwood dome trimmed in a swirling pattern, which when viewed from an upstairs window looks like a fancy dessert, right down to the tuft of box that looks like a cherry on top. Elsewhere on the property, hedges and topiary provide bold statements. Paths are edged in rows of round miniature boxwood; parterres lead to a sunken

terrace, where a pair of giant boxwoods, pruned in a dimpled pattern, flank the entrance.

Hollies are another favorite southern shrub. With their thorny leaves, hollies are an effective deterrent against trespassers and escape-prone children. They are a good choice if you live along a busy road, or your property borders a sidewalk. Hollies also offer the bonus of their festive berries and greenery at the holidays. Pyracantha, also known as firethorn, is a less popular but quite elegant choice, especially when mixed with other shrubs and allowed to follow its arching habit, and offers plentiful, showy berries. Other good choices include hornbeam, barberry, Leyland cypress, privet, cherry laurel, and yew.

It is vitally important to set the right tone in the shrubbery of your garden. It should complement the degree of formality of your house and

"Any piece of land at our disposal was here before we arrived, and it will be here after we have departed. The interim is ours, for making our lives and our gardens, and we must answer for both."

—Allen Lacy

fit with the neighborhood. Nashville's Ben Page, who works on some of the grandest projects in the city, insists that his clients consider the long-term prospect for their property. He'll often allocate a large part of the budget to trees and phase in large ones over several years if the cost is prohibitive. "Old grove management," in Page's phraseology, is a core value in his landscape design.

Other landscape architects, like Mario Nievera in Palm Beach, move large trees off-site while the house is being built and then

bring them back once the house is in place. In a disposable culture like ours, it's incumbent upon every gardener to preserve the native landscape as much as possible. But it is especially important in the South, where the regional identity is so bound to the landscape. In a world of so many things we cannot change, like the popularity of Starbucks and suburban sprawl, you do have domain up to the property line. To be sure, there are many talented people working toward the preservation of our cities and towns and historic landmarks. But it is equally important that in the small choices we make in our gardens, we make responsible decisions as well.

Allen Lacy speaks eloquently of our relationship to the land in *The Inviting Garden:* "I believe . . . that [gardeners] hold it in stewardship, that it is a responsibility, not a possession. Any piece of land at our disposal was here before we arrived, and it will be here after we have departed. The interim is ours, for making our lives and our gardens, and we must answer for both."

In the pages of *Southern Accents*, we strive to highlight as many of the stalwart survivors from the past as possible, including historic houses, treasured traditions, and timeless style. When we show a majestic tree, proudly presiding like an elder statesman over a beautifully designed new garden, we salute the enduring soul of the South.

Opposite: Boxwood can be modeled like artist's clay to create expressions of form and color. A Virginia parterre displays its tidy formations near the house. **Above:** A majestic kapok tree is a defining element in a Florida garden, speaking of the past and reaching its generous branches into the future.

CHAPTER FOUR

TROPICAL GARDENS

In the southernmost reaches of the South is its most exceptional gardening region, the tropics. With almost no winter to speak of, the lower portions of Florida and the Texas coast permit gardening year-round. The climate may set the tropical South apart, but the flamboyant style of gardening contributes to the sense that the tropical zones might as well be in another country altogether. With the spiky heads of palm trees, the vividly colored flowers, and oversized blooms, the landscape of south Florida

Opposite: A Palm Beach pool provides a dramatic reflection of exotic palms and plantings.
Above: At the entrance to a Coconut Grove, Florida, courtyard a 'Don Juan' rose, which tolerates the tropical heat and humidity, climbs the arched gateway.

Below left: Tropical thunbergia dangles romantically from a pergola in a Coconut Grove garden, providing dense shade for the lounging area beneath it. Below right: The thunbergia blossoms wave in the breeze like festive streamers. Opposite: Cuban royal and King Alexander palms salute the blue sky in this Coconut Grove, Florida, garden.

resembles a cartoon in comparison to its demure northern neighbors. Each year, we like to present a spectacular tropical garden in *Southern Accents*, usually in our January issue. These tropical gardens, with their fresh colors and lush atmosphere, always seem especially welcome during the winter doldrums. They provide hope that somewhere life does go on, that there is color in the world, and blue skies.

It is this fantastical atmosphere that makes south Florida so alluring as a winter getaway from northern cities. What could be a greater contrast to snow-blanketed Chicago than, say, a

terrace overlooking Biscayne Bay, dripping with bougainvillea and shaded by coconut palms?

Oddly, much of what forms our notions of the Florida landscape is not native to the region. Early Florida gardeners imported plants that could adapt to the climate, planting them in whatever Mediterranean or Latin American style they desired. These plants that, while not indigenous to the region, flourish there nonetheless have become synonymous with tropical style — palms from the Pacific islands, podocarpus from Africa, bougainvillea from Brazil. Exotic plants make up a great portion of

the Florida garden vocabulary, contributing to the otherworldly quality of the region.

The bones of a tropical garden are its trees. Like the Spanish moss–draped live oaks in coastal regions of the South, the palm tree gives you an immediate clue as to your whereabouts. A palm-lined avenue will inevitably evoke the great pleasure capitals of the world. With their jaunty crowns, palms are at once graceful and a bit silly, like a Dr. Seuss character. They certainly rearrange your expectations, promising fun and frivolity and perhaps a bit of elegance. Unlike the sprawling deciduous trees in other parts of the country, palms are neat, tidy, and sculptural. Their presence suggests order and predictability, the perfect environment for relaxing and leaving the cares of the world behind.

Large palms like Canary Island date palms and coconut palms have a strong vertical aspect, which lends height to a formal garden. They can be used as focal points or to indicate a boundary. With their bare trunks, they provide a canopy over lower plantings without competing on the ground level. Framed by shrubs, a large palm forms a natural sculpture, standing out against the green foliage with its silvery brown, textured trunk.

Smaller palms like the areca fill in the middle level of a garden with their dense glossy fronds, adding an exotic flair at eye level. A pathway lined with areca palms feels extremely

private and removed from the world. When a breeze stirs a palm stand, the resulting whisper and sway of the fronds contribute to the dreamy atmosphere. In a restored garden in Palm Beach, landscape architect Jorge Sanchez created an allée of areca palms. A stone runlet down the center of the allée carries your eye along the walls of the palms to the quiet vista of a low stone fountain.

Taken out of their tropical context, palms disply an exotic flair wherever they're planted. Some, like the blue fan palm and the cabbage palm, can tolerate temperatures below freezing.

Left: The owners of this Coconut Grove house wanted a Provençal feel, with olive jars, blue shutters, and a rose garden. Opposite: A walkway leads mysteriously into a thicket, around an orchid tree planted with red anthuriums, pink and white begonias, pentas, and spiky Everglades palms.

Repeated freezing will likely burn the leaves, which is reparable, or damage the crown, which is usually fatal. There are instances of palms surviving in such unlikely locations as London and Edinburgh.

These British palms no doubt date to the rage for exotic plants that consumed the English gardening world during the Victorian years. The craze gave rise to the proliferation of greenhouses and conservatories and dovetailed with the fashion for all things exotic — in attire and home design as well. As early as 1838, a palm house existed at Bicton in Devon.

In addition to palms, there are other mainstays of the tropical tree world. Kapoks are certainly the most otherworldly tree in the tropical garden, with their massive, swirling trunks. Large enough to accommodate a grown man, the sweeping folds of the kapok's aerial

roots provide a dramatic backdrop to nearly any planting. Native to India and Pakistan, the banyan is another tree that, although not native to Florida, certainly has become a standard feature in grand south Florida gardens.

Banyan trees, which can grow to ninety feet tall and are considered sacred in their native land, are a boon to tropical gardens because of the dense shade they produce under their evergreen canopies. Whenever possible, they should be considered sacred to the southern tropical garden as well and preserved at all cost. Mario Nievera removes trees from the property when there's large-scale building to be done, bringing them back when the disturbance is over.

The shrubs of a tropical garden add to the overall structure with their dense growing habit and ability to screen an area. They are especially

Above: A majestic entrance through a ficus-arched gateway proceeds down a broad area of well-manicured palms. **Opposite:** In an elegant Palm Beach garden, the formal aspects of columns and arches are echoed by a colonnade of foxtail palms leading to the pool. Landscape architect Mario Nievera planted the palms in a forced perspective, each one a little farther out, for the allée to appear longer.

useful to shield a swimming pool from neighbors and passersby. Ficus and podocarpus are two popular shrubs used in tropical landscapes, pruned to contribute to the formal garden or allowed to grow loosely in a jungle setting.

Shaped into an obelisk, a podocarpus can add a powerful vertical thrust to the essentially flat aspect of a formal garden. Trimmed into hedges, ficus creates the walls of outdoor garden rooms. Growing up to twenty feet tall, they can create a completely private space or simply screen one area of a garden from the next. Jorge Sanchez of the Palm Beach landscape firm Sanchez & Maddux likes to see them pruned in creative ways, in waves or ridges, and loves to carve doorways through their branches. He even uses ficus to create an archway over a formal entrance gate, marrying shrubbery to metal.

Between the azure of the sky overhead and the aqua of swimming pools and the ocean, shrubs establish the garden through color. Against the bleached-out hues of sand and water, the green of a garden pops out with dazzling clarity. Like an oasis in the desert, a tropical garden should make you feel cooler just by looking at it. Lush and verdant, with the soothing, light-absorbing grass and shrubs, a tropical garden can provide respite from the heat and glare of the tropical environment. Even the sound of shrubbery whispering to itself in a breeze has a cooling effect.

Contributing to the coolness of the tropical garden are the water elements. In addition to actually cooling the air, water in motion gives the illusion of moving the air, creating a breeze and stirring the stillness. Swimming pools appear in virtually all the tropical gardens we present in *Southern Accents*. They obviously serve a recreational purpose, but they fulfill an aesthetic one as well. With their shimmery, slippery surfaces, pools provide a contrast to the lush texture of plants. Gleaming in the sunshine, they add a dimension of reflection to the play of light and shadow in the garden. Situated between a house and a natural body of water, they link the civilized world to the natural one and echo the watery expanse nearby.

In limited spaces, landscape designers come up with inventive ways to shoehorn a pool into

Below left: In Peggy Sewell's Dallas garden, tropical elements lend an exotic feeling to the temperate zone. A bamboo thicket shrouds a stairway. Below right: A creeping fig-covered wall decorated with orchids in wire baskets brightens a corner of a Palm Beach garden. Opposite: Around the pool, exotic plantings heighten the sense of enclosure and privacy.

Opposite: Guests reach the front door by skirting a lily pond accented with a low water jet, which greets them with the cooling splash of water. **Right:** A garden shaded by palms and cooled by a fountain is an oasis in hot weather.

a garden. Mario Nievera minimizes the size of a long lap pool by inserting planted beds at intervals down its length. Jorge Sanchez balances the breadth of pools with vertical elements like palm trees and pergolas. He also uses checkerboard patterns of grass and stone to soften the transition between the pool and the garden. Irregularly shaped pools can fit into the tiniest of gardens and create the feeling of an exotic lagoon.

Fountains are a welcome addition to the tropical garden with the music of their cheerful splashing. In a formal tropical garden, a classical fountain can reinforce the reference to the gardens of Europe. It can create excitement and anticipation of what lies beyond, like the massive circular fountain in a spectacular Renaissance-inspired garden in Palm Beach, which lies midway between the house and the Intracoastal Waterway, providing a link between the two.

A more casual fountain can add a charming accent to an intimate courtyard, muffling the noise of the outside world and serving as a secret focal point in a sheltered nook. Its lulling music can even make you forget, however momentarily, your own troubles. Fountains also attract colorful birds whose plumage adds color to the tropical garden and offers further distraction from daily concerns.

The effect of a fountain is largely dependent on the way the water is moved. A row of

jets sending slim arcs of water over a broad pool creates an energetic atmosphere, full of festive formality. A lazy trickle brings a restful feeling to a garden, lulling your senses with its gentle, persistent burble. A powerful fountain, shooting high into the air, draws attention to itself and any garden ornament it might adorn. In creating the atmosphere of a garden, never underestimate the impact of a well-placed, properly scaled fountain.

As essential to the tropical garden as a water feature are bold flowers. The flowering plants in a tropical garden are like jewelry on a Palm Beach socialite — big and unembarrassed. The plate-size blossoms of hibiscus open hungrily to the sun, making big splashes of color in the garden. It is easy to see, gazing upon them, where Lily Pulitzer got the inspiration for her lively prints. The otherworldly quality of bromeliads, looking like nothing so much as creatures from another planet, contributes to a

feeling of complete escape from the familiar world. Orchids dangling from tree trunks seem to have reversed the usual order of things.

Under the bright sun, pale colors tend to wash out, so bright flowers serve a practical purpose, standing up to the bleaching efforts of the sun. They also show up against the pale colors of coquina stone and stucco, two popular building materials in coastal regions. A vine like allamanda, with its glossy dark leaves and big yellow flowers, can soften the hard edges of a house while brightening it as well. It complements the turquoise of a swimming pool and makes a definite statement against the deep green of palms and hedges.

Orchids are perhaps the most popular tropical plants at the moment, with good reason. There are countless varieties — including a wealth of rare ones — to be sought out

from growers, and their vivid hues and graceful growing habit make them welcome indoors and out. Set in the tropical environment, they seem to epitomize the exuberant forms of exotic plant life.

But aside from all practical considerations, these showy flowers contribute another quality to the tropical garden. With their intoxicating scents, look-at-me colors, and suggestive forms, they are, if you'll pardon me, sexy. There, now we've said it. And no intimate warm-weather garden would be complete without a little hint of sexiness. What if, on a moonlit stroll after a romantic seaside dinner, there were no fragrant blossoms for your beloved to pluck and tuck behind your ear? These gaudy, luscious flowers are as essential to the tropical experience as sunshine.

It is the differences you notice when you

Opposite left: Angel's trumpet contributes its colorful, velvety blossoms in the courtyard. **Opposite right:** The white hibiscus is a favorite tropical shrub, with a long blooming season. **Below:** A fountain and colorful plantings draw the eye across the pool and through a colonnade.

Below: A Palm Beach gardener grows orchids in baskets outdoors year-round.
Opposite: With their flagrant colors and complex blossoms, orchids epitomize the tropical flower.

Tropical Plants

- Palms
- Bougainvillea
- Allamanda
- Passion vine
- Cycads
- Tree fern
- Coconut palm
- Royal poinciana
- Leiconia
- Bromeliad
- Orchid

water features. And still, it possesses that southern character in different garb. It is bright and bold, and yet very private. It is at once stimulating and peaceful. It is simple and, on examination, amazingly complex. It is orderly but, given a moment without tending, would revert to unfathomable wilderness. It is perhaps this delicate balance that is so appealing about a tropical garden. Like the southern spirit, it seems indestructible and yet is at heart a precious and fragile thing.

visit a tropical climate. In a tropical garden, even the fauna is strange. Lizards, frogs, scorpions, and birds with assertive plumage populate this world. Dozing in the sun, the lizard embodies the lazy pace of a tropical day. Yet when disturbed, it'll skitter away in a rustle of leaves, vanishing in an instant. In the cool, shady spots, you'll find creatures seeking respite from the heat, always tucked away. The feeling of being watched is powerful in a tropical garden, perhaps because of the unseen presence of these silent companions.

Whether a tropical garden takes shape in a Victorian style or as a Renaissance ode in architectural forms or as a dramatic fantasyland of surprising juxtapositions, it is distinguished from all other southern gardens by its plant life, its seasonless life cycle, and its ever present

CHAPTER FIVE

GARDEN ORNAMENTATION

No proper southern garden exists without some type of ornamentation — be it as grand as a Roman statue or as modest as a sturdy clay pot. Both act as punctuation in a space that can be overrun by nature at any time. Dating back to ancient Egypt and becoming a fashion statement during the Renaissance, garden ornamentation has a long tradition in both Western and Eastern cultures. France mastered the incorporation of statuary into a regimented garden landscape at Vaux-le-Vicomte and Versailles. Japan, with its

Opposite: In Birmingham, Alabama, a nineteenth-century cherub frolics above a lily pond. The seating area to the right provides an ideal spot for enjoying the sound of trickling water and taking in the scent of fresh herbs. **Above:** Creeping fig that grows around a monstrous fountain softens its frightening grimace.

abiding appreciation of the untamed landscape, balanced the beauty of ornamentation with a desire to live in harmony with the landscape. Southern gardens, which are full of architectural remnants, furniture, containers, and statuary, take their cue mostly from European precedents. But the southern gardener uses these accents to develop a unique vocabulary, one that's as fluent in the past as it is mindful of the present.

Because the idea of ornamentation is so broad (it can even include plantings), it seems worthwhile to restrict the term for our pur-

poses to sculptural applications. There are stone and marble statues, terra-cotta pots, iron furniture, and even architectural remnants. And they all have their place in a cultivated plot of land: to serve as a focal point at the end of an allée, to hold plantings, to furnish an outdoor room, to draw attention or create a surprise where a plant or blossom will not. And they also add age, integrity, and sometimes character to a space governed more by forces beyond our control than those within. Ben Page, a Nashville landscape architect, says that ornamentation "brings a pivotal moment when the sculpture and the garden come together. It creates an evocative space that reflects the owner, and it makes any design sing." According to George Plumptre, author of *Garden Ornament: Five Hundred Years of History and Practice,* "man has been a creature of aspiration and herein lies the impetus for garden ornament. Ornament has elevated the garden from being a place of production to being a place of pleasure."

The variety of ornamentation appearing in gardens is so vast that it is almost dizzying. A fine neoclassical statue may look inappropriate where the craft of the month from Martha Stewart will look right at home. A nineteenth-century maiden might be more seemly than a spritely nymph. Scale, tone, and age all affect the choices when furnishing a garden with anything other than organic materials — as

Above: An antique English basin with quatrefoil banding provides the basis for the cherubic fountain. The pea gravel surrounding the fountain underscores the formal feel of the courtyard and slows you down so you can enjoy all its elements. **Opposite:** A cut stone pathway leads visitors from the driveway to the formal garden. Two dogs flanking the garden lend an air of majesty to the diminutive space.

does the architecture of the home. A modern exterior will probably be surrounded by innovative landscape design that challenges tradition. Sculpture and other ornamentation will probably be more abstract than figurative. A traditional Georgian-inspired property will communicate all the order and hierarchy inherent in the style, and the ornamentation will lean toward the neoclassical. Similarly, Victorian cottages are more likely to be surrounded by charming animals and maybe a maiden or two. Of course, there is no law that says the architecture of a house need dictate the ornamentation for the garden. However, it stands to reason that if Georgian architecture appeals, its ornamentation will also.

More than any other type of ornamentation, statuary conveys personality in a garden. The personality may communicate itself through a literal replica of the gardener or through more subtle touches — such as a favorite mythological character or a sweet cherub. It's worthwhile to reflect thoroughly and choose carefully, lest you convey a message contrary to your true desire. Aphrodite would probably not be the statuary of choice in a convent courtyard.

The type of garden also affects the choices of statuary. A statuary garden might have a collection of objects culled from a certain time period or medium or style or artist or subject matter. Sometimes statuary gardens are part of a grand formal garden; sometimes they are what they are: sculpture gardens. And often in the South, a garden might have one piece of statuary or sculpture that is prized and pivotal to the landscape — a starting point or a final flourish.

Ranging from actual antiquities and reproductions of classical figures to nineteenth-century romantic imagery to folk art objects, statues interspersed throughout an outdoor space can echo a tone that is set more subtly through plantings. What better tribute to the strength and majesty of a long allée of trees or boxwoods than a statue of Apollo surveying the line? A spirited fountain benefits from the addition of frolicking putti. Statuary of the classical sort underscores the age of the materials they're surrounded by and provides a compelling textured contrast. Most of the statuary we think of is Greek- or Roman-inspired. Oddly enough, any gardens that existed in Greece were probably dedicated to gods and not meant for mortal pleasure. Nevertheless, it is those figures that are resurrected most often in our own

landscapes. Their reasons for being, initially, were probably allegorical. Today, they may still be allegorical, or perhaps it is a matter of simple aesthetics. We often see birdbaths with a statue of Saint Francis of Assisi and other figures whose stories are sculpted into stone. They may adorn church gardens, public spaces, and even private gardens.

A lover of eighteenth-century Georgian and Regency antique furniture may disperse classical figures throughout the landscape. Someone whose interests lean more toward the Victorian might like a nineteenth-century stone statue of a shepherd carrying a lost sheep. And collectors today are also gaining an appreciation for art created by artists who work outside the typical art-world spheres. Known as outsider artists, these usually

Opposite: Doves by artist Ann Robinson evoke the Middle Ages, when rustic architectural elements were used frequently. The lush grassy path adds to the pastoral quality of the garden room, and the boxwoods that separate the rustic fence inject a lighthearted touch into the arrangement. Below left: At a Nashville estate called Watersmeet, a brick wall crowned by statuary (presumably brought over from Europe in the 1930s by landscape architect Bryant Fleming) marks the passage from one garden area to another. A wildflower garden is in close proximity, proving that formal landscape design and informal plantings can coexist in a garden. Below right: Eighteenth-century portrait sphinxes refer back to ancient Egypt, but the French reproductions were usually commissioned works that depicted their owners' mistresses. This particular sphinx sits before the front door in a Nashville garden. Below, bottom: A Celtic cross in the pathway marks the entry to Glen Burnie's gardens.

Following pages: (left) A wall of papyrus creates a background of greenery and, in some way, restrains the spirited antics of the three cavorting boys in a Greensboro, North Carolina, garden. (right) When designing a formal garden, walls are a necessity, particularly if the garden butts up to a neighboring property. While stone walls are lovely, a redbrick wall is a good colorful backdrop for statuary, particularly if the statue is made of lead or stone.

Left: An iron fawn at Watersmeet stands at attention as you pass from one garden room to the terrace.

untrained people create works that incorporate found and fantastic objects in a naive but always thought-provoking way.

In the South, because the architecture tends toward the neoclassical, our formal gardens are overwhelmingly adorned with objects of classical inspiration. In smaller gardens and in enclosed garden spaces, putti appear frequently. The diminutive cherubs, who are as full of mirth as they are charm, capture the spirit of the landscape — its untamed nature balanced by its obvious beauty. Most often they can be found in fountains, but they also appear surrounded by a blanket of greenery, be it ivy or some other enveloping growth.

Deities are another matter. They evoke their Roman forebears even though most that have made it across the Atlantic were produced in the nineteenth and early twentieth centuries. They are made from lead, stone, marble, or bronze. And they bear the patina of age. Most are life-size or a little larger and may communicate as much about the garden's owner as they do about the garden itself. In order for a garden to support such substantive statuary, it must be mature and is usually more formal.

Of course, finding and caring for a recog-

nized deity is a challenge in today's collecting market. It is much easier and sometimes more desirable to seek out sprites and nymphs, sphinxes, and minor gods. They are much more appropriate to intimate spaces and small gardens and are also more prevalent on the market. In Nashville, Ben Page placed an antique sphinx near a doorway and covered it with greenery. According to Page, sphinxes were often created with the face of the homeowner's mistress. "It's amazing," he says. "Many of the faces are so distinct that they would be recognizable." In this garden, the sphinx is not only an object of beauty but also a subject of amusement for those who know its checkered history. The fact that the sphinx is so well crafted that the face seems recognizable — the model passed away years before, of course — is one mark of quality.

It is the faces in antiques and reproductions that distinguish the most compelling statuary. As noted earlier, statuary personalizes a garden. But the face, the expression in a statue, seems particularly communicative. A goblin spews forth water from his angry mouth in a Dallas garden. The effect would be frightening were not the face so eloquently old and powerful. At Glen Burnie in Winchester, Virginia, an ivy-ensconced figure peers out from his post next to the entrance gate. The effect in the garden is one of surprise and pleasure. He almost invites you to get as lost among the myriad plantings as he is.

Above: At Glen Burnie in Winchester, Virginia, a nineteenth-century face — purported to be an English barrister — peers out over the ivy and English daylilies at its feet. The face is actually an entire bust, but the ivy has taken over. The gate to the left marks the passage to the family cemetery.

Opposite and right: Commissioned from an artist in Mexico, this immense statue of a woman looks as if it were rescued from a centuries-old site. "A wimpy piece of sculpture would be lost at that site," says Nashville landscape architect Ben Page.

As with many of the grand houses throughout the United States, Glen Burnie's landscape includes various garden rooms, one of which is a statuary garden. Populated mostly with figures from classical antiquity, the combination of tamed landscape and sculpted stone is powerful. Though the garden was constructed almost fifty years ago, its grand collection of statuary and majestic plantings make the garden feel as if it's been in existence for even longer than the house. The landscape is designed with long shrub- and flower-bordered allées that underscore the impressiveness of the statuary. While it is the plantings themselves that make the garden great, the statuary communicates the idea that this is an important garden, thoughtfully planned out and carefully crafted.

In great gardens, large and small, fountains seem to be an integral part. In fact, fountains topped by anything from putti to Hercules are often the only statuary in small gardens. The constancy of water, the steadfastness of stone, and the eternal presence of the landscape all convey the timelessness of our environment. The house may crumble and fade, but the landscape, with all its elements, will always exist.

Of course, where statuary is concerned, there is some limit to its durability — particularly in our society in which environmental hazards such as pollution can damage them. So reproduction as well as new statuary often take the place of

more fragile antique examples. Ben Page commissioned an enormous head of a woman for the Nashville garden with the sphinx. The antique and new work coexist well because the latter was artificially aged and given a patina similar to that of the former. The head, which lies on its side, was placed before a view of the landscape beyond. It resembles a figurehead taken from the bow of a ship, but the scale is immense, too large for such a role. Its size makes it seem as if it were resurrected from some ancient temple and thus underscores the age and maturity of the garden, as well as the house.

Much of the statuary we see now is eigh-teenth- and nineteenth-century, when artisans became increasingly interested in the human form. Neoclassicism became popular during the eighteenth century as artists tried to replicate the statues of classical antiquity — mastering the form of the human body, draping fabric over the figure of a woman to reveal a thigh or breast, emphasizing the musculature of a man. During the nineteenth century, a growing

Below: An eighteenth-century stone statue of Prometheus stands at the end of a rose-lined allée. **Opposite above:** A limestone statue of Actaeon stands at the end of the Grand Allée at Glen Burnie. Bordering the allée are flowering crab apple trees. **Opposite below:** Thirty-two Hatfield yews provide a background for the terra-cotta bust of Julius Ceasar.

puritanism seemed to be at war with what had happened a century earlier. So less revealing pastoral figures such as maidens and shepherds appeared as often as mythological figures.

Animals were another answer to a growing puritanical sentiment. They are occasionally actual replicas of favorite pets, but specific portrait or not, dogs, horses, or turtles, the variety is limitless. Lead dogs may stand at attention and flank an entrance to a courtyard; a verdigris horse may stand alone in contrast

with the surrounding greenery; a turtle may look into a small pond contemplating whether to slip in for dip. Animal statuary can convey formality or a little frivolity. It depends on the quality and the expression of each object.

In a garden, greenery is not the only background for statuary. An architectural element can also provide an evocative contrast. In a small garden the side of a house may offer an easy surface on which to train ivy or other climbing greenery. A freestandng iron gate or redbrick wall may help trained shrubbery delineate a garden room. The backdrop you choose for any piece of sculture will enhance the implied importance of that piece of sculpture. After all, you light the art you have in your home. A carefully selected frame surrounds a prized painting. A pedestal supports a unique piece of sculpture. The art that fills a garden deserves the same consideration and attention. It's one thing to plant ivy or even design plantings around outdoor statuary; it's another to construct a stucco or brick wall. Because statuary is an investment, and a landscape does not just develop overnight, the greatest chore and pleasure in creating a garden is choosing statuary that will stand the test of time and weather.

Ornament for ornamentation's sake in the garden communicates a more subtle message. Perhaps the garden is less ordered than one filled with statuary

Following pages: Punctuating the flat parterre garden space is a vertical obelisk, which adds an architectonic element to the composition. Bought in 1910, dating to the eighteenth century, this obelisk follows a tradition begun by the Egyptians, coopted by the Romans, and reused from the Renaissance to today.

Below left: Iron urns from the nineteenth century may mark the steps on a grand staircase or greet you at the end of a long allée. Their weathered patina creates a striking contrast to a lush blanket of greenery and the ecru color of stone. Below middle: A hand-carved urn of Vicenza stone marks a pathway that leads to a vintage scalloped concrete urn and then on to the woods beyond. Below right: The reproduction ram's head urn features traditional motifs. With a little exposure to the elements, it will take on all the color and character of an antique from another century. Opposite: Combining architecture and landscape, an open windowsill holds a nineteenth-century French cast-iron urn.

or is more receptive to the dictates of nature, willing to be subject to it rather than dominate it. Symbolic obelisks, architectural remnants, and innovative containers all lend a personal touch to an outdoor environment without projecting an individual face. They also speak to the continuum of time, as they stand true and the environment around them is ever changing.

Obelisks are a particular favorite among southern gardeners. Inspired by ancient Egypt and rediscovered by Napoleon during his forays into that country, they continue to be produced today. Because of their height and structure, they serve as a focal point in a parterre garden or as a beacon in a less manicured area. They refer back to antiquity, but their beauty continues to appeal today as a bit of abstract sculpture in an area dominated by nature.

It's uncertain how long architectural remnants have been used in the landscape. Their function in the beginning may have been practical. An old column provides a tall, solid support for a growing vine; window frames create an interesting framework for blossoms. As time has passed, our appreciation for the aesthetic order conveyed by columns and capitals in a garden has matched their usefulness in architecture.

But the most versatile of all garden ornamentation has to be the urn. As useful as they are beautiful, urns appear often in the pages of *Southern Accents*. They may take the form of terra-cotta containers or olive jars or iron, bronze, or stone vessels. But their shape is infinitely appealing; their roles in a garden, myriad; and their history, long.

Opposite: Seating in a garden provides a moment to pause and reflect. This early-nineteenth-century semicircular bench, which sits in a Nashville garden, came from Louisiana. It fills part of a round terrace that sits at the end of a long allée. **Right:** A rustic demi-gazebo provides an ideal location for an afternoon repast. The walls are open to allow air to circulate. Tall trees overhead lend the necessary shade. **Below:** A weathered antique iron bench holds a permanent spot on a Birmingham terrace for surveying the garden beyond.

An urn is, after all, a container. It can be moved to take advantage of light and air. It can be filled from season to season with different flowers. Eighteenth- and nineteenth-century stone and metal urns are often sculptural works of art in themselves. Actually filling them with flowers is a little like icing the cake. In pairs, they may flank steps within the garden or from the garden to the house. More rustic containers such as olive jars are rarely filled because their form and size make it unnecessary. And urns, like all other garden ornamentation, can be used inside — in a garden room or living room, for that matter.

Stone urns, like statuary, often begin neutral in color but take on a greenish hue as moss

creeps into place. The effect can be damaging, but the patina implied is often quite lovely. Whether to keep the moss becomes a conservation issue, but its existence is often quite desirable, for it conveys both age and a communication with the landscape that is particularly captivating in a garden.

Southern Accents garden essayist Lee May says that he always likes a bench in a garden, some place to sit and contemplate either the beauty around him or something more profound. The types of furniture that might fill a garden are widely varied, distinct as an antique stone table or a new teak wood chaise longue. Both functional and frivolous, insofar as it is designed to accent a garden, furniture provides yet another means to personalize an outdoor space.

Both grand and intimate gardens are often broken up into smaller rooms, where a gardener can experiment with different plantings. Such rooms may be accented by statuary or ornament, but the most pleasant are furnished with a bench or chairs and a table. Alfresco dining is one of the pleasures of living in the South, and most gardens are equipped to take advantage of every

Opposite: At Glen Burnie, a cast-iron statue of Triton holds a conch shell above his left shoulder. Water cascades from the shell over a rock formation surrounded by a scallop shell.

opportunity. Ideal for luncheons or cocktails, an outdoor table provides a way for others to enjoy your gardening efforts. From a practical perspective, relatively new furniture is the most useful, and examples designed to incorporate the landscape make you feel a part of it.

But antique benches and tables have their own function and aesthetics. They may not invite the same languorous repose — they do not come with cushions — but they provide a quiet moment for stopping and appreciating the landscape. Further, they are works of art in and of themselves. With sculpted decorative motifs from centuries past and the patina of years of outdoor exposure, antique outdoor furniture has a definite place in the contemporary garden.

Conservation

- Antique garden ornaments made from bronze should be cleaned regularly. Use soft brushes to remove dirt and debris. Use cotton cloths and a nonsudsing detergent such as Ivory dishwashing detergent in water.

- Lead ornaments are affected most by organic acids produced by debris, decaying leaves, and bird droppings. To clean, use a nonsudsing detergent and water.

- Stone statuary can absorb moisture from the ground. It is best to have a barrier between the ground and statuary. Use a soft brush and nonsudsing detergent to clean.

- Carnuba, a non-silicon-based natural tree wax, can be used on bronze and lead statuary to prevent decomposition. Carnuba wax can be purchased at most hardware stores.

- Ornamentation suffers most from intense sunlight, lichen, moss, and lawn equipment (i.e., lawn mowers and weed eaters).

- Replacing broken appendages or pieces of antique garden ornaments is not recommended. Repairs can cause more problems than the actual break. It is important to consider the amount of stress the repair will cause on the statuary. Don't make repairs that you can't undo in the future.

- When transporting antique ornaments overseas, make sure the statuary is enclosed in some type of waterproof material. Ask the shipping company about air-conditioned compartments or devices that give detailed reports on the temperature or angles the statuary may have been stored at during transport. It is important to avoid rapid changes in humidity.

- Some sensible advice on purchasing antique garden ornamentation: (1) go through a reputable firm; (2) have a conservator give you a condition report of the statuary before purchasing; (3) as insurance, make photos before packing and shipping; (4) take extra care in the preservation and maintenance process.

- For information regarding specific antique statuary or maintenance and preservation, contact the American Institute for Conservation of Historic and Artistic Works in Washington, D.C., 202/452-9545. For overseas inquiries call the International Institute for Conservation of Historic and Artistic Works in London at 44-171-839-5975.

Below left: Grand southern estates are often named, and their vintage signage can become a compelling part of a garden arrangement. Stonehill House in Columbus, Georgia, is surrounded by ten acres of perennials and roses. Below middle: A bronze statue of Diana stands amid yellow columbine and prepares to send her arrow toward a profusion of 'New Dawn' roses in the garden at Stonehill House. Below right: Once a church steeple, now a makeshift obelisk, this object echoes the strong vertical elements through the Little Rock garden. Opposite: Bronze fennel fans the skirt of a nineteenth-century statue of Phoebe.

Often gardens are designed around a piece of furniture, particularly if it is unique. A rounded bench might fill part of a rondel in a landscape. A petite stool might bring down the scale of plantings in a garden room. Because antique garden furniture is so extraordinary and hard to come by, pieces are often found before the landscape is designed — and the two are destined to exist happily together.

Of course, bad ornamentation cannot be rectified by even the most magnificent landscape. Where statuary is concerned, the value is not assigned only on quality of design. The material, the craftsmanship, and the beauty of the individual piece make the marriage of landscape to figure succeed.

Plastic has no place in the garden — even at a lawn party. The same applies to ornament and furniture. The materials that make up every accent in a landscape should imply timelessness, even if they were installed only a few months earlier. Of course, reproductions are very useful in a garden because they can take the place of a stone sculpture whose time in the sun has passed. The challenge is to always look at the quality of the artistry as well as the quality of the object. You look at proportion, craftsmanship, and details when judging whether to buy a house or a piece of furniture. The same criteria apply to statuary. And in contrast to a home or piece of furniture, the landscape endures — and so should its ornamentation.

CHAPTER SIX

WATER FEATURES

Water features are utterly necessary in southern gardens, providing cool respite from the heat of the day and highlighting the formal bones of the garden or emphasizing its meandering woodland quality. Whether classical or casual, most water features have been inspired by great historical water features around the world. As with so much of southern design, this element of the garden stays mindful of the past while stepping confidently into the future.

Looking out over a piazza in the middle of Rome, a

Opposite: Japanese blood grass provides a strong vertical contrast to the horizontal stones surrounding the pond in Sally Reynolds's water garden in Brentwood, Tennessee. **Above:** Koi give a pool infinite movement and variety.

Below: Donna Hackman added a woodland garden to her Middleburg, Virginia, property as a second phase of planning and attracted an entirely new group of wildlife with the new habitat. **Opposite above:** The woodland landscape at Glen Burnie, a historic estate in Winchester, Virginia, benefits from a natural waterfall. **Opposite below:** In the grotto an aged cast-iron fountain, streaked with rust, has encouraged the thick growth of moss over the years.

marble figure of Oceanus lifts one imperious hand above the Trevi Fountain and commands the waters to flow. Sheeting over the edge of rocky pools, sparkling in the spray of jetting fountains, the water is noisy, jubilant, and extravagant. In the center of a terrace on a majestic Palm Beach estate, a small fountain featuring a cavorting putti provides a striking focal point to gardens taking direct inspiration from Renaissance Italy. In its diminutive way more appropriate for the site, the Palm Beach fountain pays tribute to the Trevi and captures the Italian spirit in a grand manner.

In a Middleburg, Virginia, garden, water

falls in a series of shallow cascades between clusters of bluebells and irises contained between banks of natural stone. Dappled with sunlight, a shining seam in a wooded landscape, the water is alive and ever changing, molded by the garden around it. Whether it falls from the sky or bubbles up out of the earth, whether cupped in a seashell or tumbling in a mighty cascade, water is a gift. The life-giving element that sets Earth apart from the rest of the solar system, it covers more than 75 percent of our planet and makes up more than 60 percent of the human body. "Water is a living thing," wrote Chinese landscape painter Kuo Hsi in the eleventh century, "hence its aspect may be deep and serene, gentle and smooth; it may be vast and ocean-like, winding and circling. It may be oily and shining, may spout like a fountain, shooting and splashing. It may form waterfalls rising up against the sky or dashing down to the deep earth; it may delight the fishermen, making the trees and grass joyful; it may be charming in the company of mist and clouds or gleam radiantly, reflecting the sunlight in the valley. Such is the living aspect of water."

Water in the garden — whether a turquoise swimming pool, a woodland pond, or a tiny birdbath — can evoke the garden's deepest life force, the thing that Virgil calls the "in-dwelling spirit of nature." Ancient visions of paradise always included water, from Buddhism's celestial palace on the shores of a lily-filled lake to the

147

Left: In Dallas, Texas, an old boathouse serves as the Sewell's folly. Below: A placid stream runs through the oriental garden at Glen Burnie, providing motion in the enclosed space. Opposite: Clipped boxwoods in pots lend an Italianate air to the terrace pond in Peggy Sewell's garden.

Gardens of Paradise — "the Gardens underneath which rivers flow" — described in the Koran. A garden is a little earthly paradise, and the water punctuating the garden landscape reminds us of the central importance of water in the world. In the famous gardens of Katsura Palace in Kyoto, paths lead through gardens built around a lake and its island, connected by bridges. Although the garden is not large, it gives the sense of a whole enclosed universe, each vista revealing another detail, and each detail — a teahouse, a boulder, a stand of bamboo reflected in a quiet inlet — revealing more about the world.

Translated to another climate and topography, the same principles hold firm: the twenty-five-acre gardens at Glen Burnie in Winchester, Virginia, unfold in a series of clipped hedges, hidden garden rooms, and formal walks that gently modulate into a naturalistic landscape half shaded by a canopy of maples. Created by a descendant of the estate's eighteenth-century founder, the garden is neither entirely historical nor entirely contemporary, borrowing from the house's formal eighteenth-century roots but preserving a timeless sense of wilderness. Nowhere is that more true than in the Water Garden, where water cascades over a stone wall into a narrow spring-fed pool banked with Japanese irises and hostas, with a simple bridge leading to a shady pavilion. Like the gardens at the Katsura Palace, the gardens at Glen Burnie seem to shut out one world while opening up another.

For all their infinite variety, all gardens follow only two basic philosophies: nature tamed or nature wild. Formal gardens have their roots in

Below: Landscape architect Jorge Sanchez planted areca palms to form an avenue leading to a focal-point fountain in the Meisters' Palm Beach garden.
Opposite: At the Colemans' house in Palm Beach, a pool provides a visual link between the indoors, a courtyard, and an espaliered wall that borders the property.

the walled gardens of ancient Persia, fruit- and flower-scented oases built around a spring in the middle of the desert. Divided into four quarters in a design called *chahar bagh*, the Persian gardens set the pattern for an orderly vision of a paradise where the unruly, chaotic side of nature submits to the tranquillity of symmetry and balance. Formal gardens built on this model take some of their beauty from the serene geometry of circles, rectangles, and squares that suggests formal grandeur even on a small scale. Even a single brick-bordered square

of clipped grass inset with a miniature fountain breathes a sense of order and rationality that can be infinitely soothing. In a Birmingham, Alabama, garden, an antiques dealer achieves maximum effect with an antique fountain set dead center in a square bed among minimal plantings. After a day spent in close examination of antique furniture, the simple power of his fountain view must be a soothing sight.

In formal gardens water is often used to provide an axis — think of the grand reflecting pool at the Taj Mahal, the long reflecting pool along Washington's Mall. It may also be used, perhaps as with a fountain or pond, to create a momentary rest in the design, as harmonious and necessary as a rest in music. Each formal garden is different, but always the gardens are divided and subdivided by clean lines and geometric shapes.

The symmetry of the Persian garden, especially as translated around the Mediterranean, is well suited to Spanish Revival architecture. In Florida — particularly along the ocean, where the intense tropical sun makes spots of bright light and pools of deep, velvety shadows — the strong, definite shapes of the formal garden show up dramatically. A diminutive raised pool lined with cobalt blue tiles in a courtyard of a Spanish Revival house in Palm Beach recalls the well of an enclosed garden in Granada or Marrakech, its mathematical symmetry delightfully interrupted with bright

Above: Outside private courtyards provide cool and peaceful spots for relaxing. **Opposite:** The owner's 400 roses encircle the classical fountain and give a pleasing view from the terrace.

flowering vines. Beyond the walls of the court-yard a double set of coquina stone steps leads to a larger ornamental pool set in concentric circles of gardens and walkways, bounded at the garden's edge with an arc of clipped hedge. At ground level the garden is a secret, orderly world, a fragrant paradise filled with the scent of roses and the gentle splash of water falling in criss-crossing jets of spray into the pool's blue depths. But from the stair landing, the larger world is visible: a sweep of grass, a natural waterway, and a dark, untamed line of trees against the sky.

Seventeeth-century French landscape architect André Le Nôtre was the first European designer to fully understand and use the power-ful tension between the tamed and the untamed in the garden. At Versailles, Le Nôtre set great basins of water in the ground and filled the near landscape with jetting fountains, mazes, and monumental statues, all the time teasing the eye down green allées toward the uncultivated world beyond the garden's borders. With all the splendid self-confidence of his patron Louis XIV, the Sun King, he dared to pierce the walls of paradise and let nature be visible.

Le Nôtre's lead was soon picked up and ampli-fied by English landscape designer William Kent. In Horace Walpole's expressive words, Kent "leaped the fence and saw that all nature was a garden," and his sensitive understanding of England's green landscape and his skillful kneading together of nature and artifice are still touchstones of garden

design. Donna Hackman followed Kent's principles in the woodland area of her massive garden in Middleburg, Virginia. Clearing out undergrowth, she revealed a charming sloping hillside. Working with talented stonemasons, she carved a narrow stream down the hillside, which spills into pools and eddies, nurturing the shade-loving wild plants and attracting new birds and other wildlife to the habitat she created.

At Rousham House near Oxford, Kent reworked an older garden to compose a series of glades and vistas at a bend in the River Cherwell. His most artful composition at Rousham is the

Left: At Sally Reynolds's water garden in Brentwood, Tennessee, a naturalistic waterfall terminates in a rock-edged pool. Opposite: A rushing waterfall complements a naturalistic garden in Tennessee. Following pages: At Tyreconnell in Baltimore, Maryland, a fountain situated beneath the terrace provides a launching point for the long descent of the hillside.

Vale of Venus, a miniature valley furnished with a series of small ponds and waterfalls. From the foot of the vale, a trick of perspective hides the ponds themselves, creating the pleasing illusion of water tumbling in a series of cascades over rough stone walls. Viewed from above, the ponds align themselves in a straight line pointing toward the river, dappled by midday light or glimmering in the shadows of approaching dusk. Mario Nievera used a similar device in his design for a series of terraces and fountains in Palm Beach. From above, they lead the eye naturally downhill toward Lake Worth. From below, the sparkling jets of water shield the house from passing boat traffic.

Natural effects can require even more planning than formal designs. The design of any natural garden is by definition dictated by its location — climate, sunlight, soil, and the physical features of the site. Water in a natural garden can be in the form of a pond, a stream, or even a bog surrounded by native stones and planted with native and wet-loving plants. But the design and maintenance of this seemingly casual type of garden requires as much attention as the rigid circles and squares of a formal garden. A pond and stream recently installed in a Brentwood, Tennessee, hillside garden, for instance, is edged with slabs of stone and piles of small rounded river rocks such as may be found in any Tennessee wilderness. And yet, nature is guided to optimal advantage where shallow cascading waterfalls spill into the stream, well within view of the terrace. Dwarf varieties of red- and green-leafed Japanese maples and arborvitae, while not native to the area, blend in with the landscape, and their diminutive size ensures that the pond — which

Below: An old lap pool in Palm Beach is sheltered by a vine-covered pergola and embellished with fanciful tile. **Opposite:** An old stone bridge, original to the property, forms an elliptical shape in the creek with its reflection.

supports a lively population of carp — will never be overshadowed by trees.

English writer Thomas Whately in his 1772 *Observations on Modern Gardening* wrote that "water accommodates itself to every situation; is the most interesting object in the landscape . . . captivates the eye at a distance, invites approach, and is delightful when near; it refreshes an open exposure; it animates a shade." He could add that water can reflect or refract; that water is infinitely cooling on a hot summer day; that it reminds us of time passing and of nature's

timeless, elemental force; that it provides a visual counterpoint to solid architecture, a yin to the yang of bricks and stone.

Bridges have their own metaphorical language of connection and movement in the landscape. Standing on a bridge and gazing down at the water, we see our own reflection and then let our imagination travel below the surface to the cool depths populated with darting fish and waving plants. Looking at a bridge from a distance (think of the famous green bridge spanning the water garden at Monet's Giverny), our sense of the surrounding landscape is sharpened and heightened. A good bridge is not an intrusion on the landscape but an integral part of the landscape's flow. At Peggy Sewell's garden in Dallas, a stone bridge over a still creek meets its reflection in a perfect ellipse — part reality, part illusion. The bridge connects the formal gardens to the untamed wilderness, a bamboo thicket on the other side of the creek. Other man-made structures — pavilions, pergolas, even a line of stepping-stones — can contribute the same gentle direction as the garden landscape, conveying a sense of stillness and permanence against the water's constant movement. In keeping with Italian-style garden design, the Sewell garden relies on detailed stonework and green plantings to convey an old-world feeling and a sense of understated elegance.

In a shady garden behind a stone Tudor house in Birmingham, Alabama, an antique

Opposite: Emily Majors Steadman designed a peaceful Birmingham garden for Robert Hill and Anthony Fant that uses water features to highlight the natural beauty of the property, like this majestic oak tree. **Right:** Large boxwoods frame the entrance to the pond terrace and separate it from the rest of the garden.

garden seat inscribes its iron filigree against a crescent of white impatiens. Seated there, the passerby can pause to enjoy the reflection of branches and sky in a serene lily pool dappled with the sunlight that filters through overarching trees. Inset in a flagstone terrace, the long rectangle of water is almost a piece of liquid architecture, a little man-made oasis. Slightly elevated, the lip of the pool holds the water above ground level to create an illusion of solidity, charmingly contrasted by half a dozen jets of water that arc from the pool's sides.

Water is a playful element and takes well to enhancement; when agitated, it sparkles and foams and is pleasing to the ear. Perhaps the world's most spectacular and engaging display of jetting waters can be found at Villa d'Este at Tivoli, east of Rome. The owners of Tyreconnell, a leafy estate near Baltimore now open to the public, brought some of the spirit of the Villa d'Este to their own Maryland landscape. The garden, designed in the 1920s and based on the Italian model, is dotted with fountains — a solitary bronze figure in a pool, a lion's head gushing water, a circle of playful stone children washed in a fan of spray. Other gardens evoke the same inventive spirit, from the weathered stone figure releasing a cascade of water down a mossy slope at Glen Burnie to a pair of putti holding up a gentle spray in a goldfish pond in Nashville to an imposing classical fountain

ringed with pristine white impatiens on a grand terrace in Palm Beach.

Who can resist a fountain, splashing, glittering, churning, foaming, its drift of spray outstretched like a pennant on a windy day? But a fountain is more than water: a fountain stands out even at a distance, whether it is an imposing piece of sculpture or a naturalistic arrangement of stones. A punctuation mark in the landscape, a beautiful fountain helps organize the rhythm of the garden, both focal point and guidepost. A fountain set in a wall in Sally Foley's garden in Georgia compels you to stop on the grassy terrace, enjoy the splash of the fountain, and perhaps take in the view the terrace affords over the rest of the garden. Fountains need not be large or elaborate to be effective: even a small fountain brings movement and sound to the garden, suggesting coolness and comfort on even the hottest day.

Below: Grass growing up to the edge of the pool makes it a decorative feature as much as a place for recreation. **Opposite:** At the Kramers' majestic Palm Beach estate, landscape architect Mario Nievera created an elegant series of outdoor spaces formally centered on classical fountains.

Different fountains create varying effects (although all have the practical advantage of aerating a pond for fish and agitating the water to keep mosquitoes from breeding). Cascading, shimmering, and sparkling, sounding even from a distance the quiet murmur of moving water, a fountain provides an almost subliminal background for our enjoyment of the garden. As we move toward it, the balance shifts and the moving water captures our attention, stimulating our sense of sound just as a bank of bright flowers stimulates our sense of sight.

The eleven fountain types identified by eighteenth-century French architect Bernard Forest de Belidor still stand as the major classifications of waterworks. The most familiar is the gravity-defying *jet d'eau*, sending a plume

of water geysering straight up into the air or, its force turned all the way down, bubbling quietly so that its movement barely disturbs the surface of the water. Tilted, the jet becomes a *berceau*, describing a bright parabola in the air — *berceaux* may water a pond or pool or, as they do in a formal fountain behind a grand Spanish Revival house in Palm Beach, shoot out in groups of three to create a sparkling envelope for a piece of bronze sculpture. Many small jets lined up together become a *grille*, a delicate veil of water; other combinations yield the *gerbe*, a sort of airy pyramid of tumbling drops; the *arbre d'eau*, a treelike branching spray; the *champignon* (mushroom), a tight glassy umbrella of water.

Some fountains are artificial waterfalls. A smooth, glazed wall of water is a *nappe* (the highly descriptive "tablecloth"), inviting to the touch. A cascade is more like a natural waterfall, deliberately fractured by the design of the structure over which the water falls. Mogul gardeners building their wondrous pleasure gardens in the foothills of the Himalayas used the abundance of natural water to invent a form of cascade called a *chadar*, or veil. Made half of sunlight, half of water, the sparkling *chadar* flows over a wide incline of shallow steps, which break the film of water into a frothy sheet. A plume can evoke the thunder of Victoria Falls or be as modest as a Japanese *tsukubai*, a hollow

Opposite: A little round fountain prepares the eye for the larger expanse of a pool in Palm Beach. **Right:** At sunset, the Colemans' pool mirrors the house's charming facade.

bamboo spigot that directs tinkling water into a small pool. A waterfall that emerges from a hidden place becomes a *grotte,* or grotto, romantic and mossy or clean and coolly modern, depending on design. Many fountain forms combined create a *théâtre d'eau,* the most ambitious of all water garden designs.

A fountain usually falls into a basin, and the basin itself can become a form of fountain. Sometimes the basin is deliberately designed with a curving lip so that the water, filled to the brim, overflows into a secondary pool or channel. In a large basin, the surface of the water may have several characters: dimpled and frothy where water falls into it, smooth and reflective where the water is still.

Whether agitated by a fountain or ruffled only by a passing breeze, a simple pool of water offers infinite possibilities in the water garden. Water is a mirror, its reflection constantly changing with the wind and light. Set in the middle of a lawn or capturing the wavering upside-down image of a sunlit facade, a pool of water adds subtle movement to a serene landscape.

The earliest pools, in Persian gardens, were built low to the ground and were severely geometrical: square, rectangular, round, or a lotuslike quatrefoil design. These pools are thought to have had a practical as well as a symbolic function — their gentle evaporation helped cool the surrounding gardens and courtyards.

Also on the practical side, water provides an

environment for plants that must grow in or near water, and a habitat for fish and an attraction for butterflies and wild birds. Unlike the other basic elements of the garden, which change over time and need constant renewal and care — soil, plants, grass — water can be used, as it were, raw. A simple lozenge of water placed in a green lawn, a straight channel of water incised through a concrete patio, can be beautiful in its classic simplicity.

Like nature itself, pools seem to abhor a vacuum — walk by a city fountain and its bottom will sparkle with thrown coins; look into a garden pool and you will almost inevitably find fish, colorful tiles, or floating plants. Gardeners who set out to create a simple pond often find themselves happily kidnapped by the process. The fish come first — who can resist the flash of koi or the more modest glimmer of

goldfish? Then come the plants to oxygenate the water for the fish, a few simple water hyacinths to begin with perhaps, but then papyrus, water lilies, and lotus. With all that greenery in the water, the banks begin to look bare, so new plantings of Japanese iris, dwarf bamboo, and ferns appear, useful to cool the water much as shade trees cool the landscape.

"Design the pond with respect to its position in the land," wrote the author of *Sakuteiki,* an eleventh-century Japanese treatise on gardening. "Follow its request, when you encounter a potential site, consider its atmosphere, think of the mountains and water of living nature and reflect constantly on such settings." For modern gardeners, freed by electric pumps and underground hydraulics to place a pond and fountain wherever they please, it can be tempting to position a pond

wherever human caprice — not Mother Nature — directs, but there are still some practical dicta that must be followed. Aquatic plants, for instance, need at least six hours of sunlight to bloom; not only may large overhanging trees shade the pond and drop troublesome leaves, but their roots can make digging the pond difficult. Consider also the vantage point from which the pond will be viewed (including, perhaps, from above, from a balcony or window). If the pool is designed to be surrounded by plants, test the soil and, if necessary, amend it before digging, or even redesign the garden so the pool will be in a more hospitable site.

Not all pools, of course, are designed to be solely decorative: a swimming pool — whether a narrow lap pool or a more expansive full-size swimming pool — can add a pleasing and practical element to the garden. Swimming pools need not be off-the-rack affairs; shaped by both landscape and nearby architecture, they can become a beautiful garden feature in themselves, binding together the garden and its structures. Clear and gemlike, they sparkle in the sun, defined at the edge perhaps with clipped boxwood hedges or plantings of bright flowers, or left unadorned and open to the sky, as severely simple as a glittering piece of modern sculpture.

Since so many of its qualities — depth, water clarity, location — are determined by its function, a swimming pool's shape becomes one of its most important design elements; but like a poet writing a sonnet, a good landscape designer can find an almost infinite range of variations within the form. Behind a Georgian-style house in Nashville, for instance, a classic rectangular pool narrows at the shallow end to a small, intimate bay defined by shallow boxwood peninsulas.

Holding the upside-down reflection of a Doric facade in Hobe Sound, Florida, a serene pool is as simple as the architecture, shaped into a classical cartouche by four inverted corners. A rectangular pool at the end of a grassy courtyard of a Spanish Revival house in Palm Beach is bordered at the edge with colorful Moorish painted tile; an adjacent round pool inset echoes the rounded arches of the distant loggia. Sometimes simplicity is the most beautiful

solution: behind another Florida house, a newly built Tuscan villa in Miami, a simple square of water bordered by stone visually links the house to the Intracoastal Waterway at the foot of the lawn. Sometimes lovely elaboration suits the site best, as in a crescent of turquoise water behind a Dallas house, dappled by sunlight and ruffled by arcing spouts.

Water and light work in concert in the garden. Garden light is never still: the sun traverses the garden by the hour, so that the

Left: The pool is set away from the Kramer house in Palm Beach across an expanse of lawn to emphasize the spaciousness of the property. Opposite: Bill Hewitt cultivates showy water lilies in his Franklin, Tennessee, garden.

same body of water may be sometimes in the cool shadows, sometimes sparkling in the sun, sometimes wavering and trembling in filtered shade. The quality of light becomes another element in garden design: deep shade; dappled shade; high midday sun; long, level rays of morning and evening. Geography plays a part in the sculpting of light and shade. The southernmost gardens of Florida and Texas receive a strong vertical light with deep shadows. Farther north in Virginia and Tennessee, the sun travels a lower path from horizon to horizon, casting long horizontal shadows for a good part of the day; in the misty high country, the light is soft; near the ocean, it can be sharp and intense.

When water is introduced into the garden, the garden itself becomes a beautiful vessel, containing and shaping the water. For its own part, water becomes a punctuation mark in the garden, poetically interrupting the flow of the ground: the garden shapes space; water amplifies it, creating a harmonious interplay of sound, light, shade, and reflection, artfully contrasting stillness and movement, exuberance and serenity. From the smallest drop of dew to the most bombastic show of the fountain-maker's art, water is an element that can't be overlooked — and once introduced, can't be ignored. Its power to nurture, to soothe, to delight, and to refresh reaches back to some of our most powerful ancestral instincts. Perhaps that's why the Koran instructs that the only word spoken in the Gardens of Paradise, the model for so many of our earthly gardens, is *peace.*

CHAPTER SEVEN

DESIGNING WITH PLANTS

Fences and walls can delineate a yard, but plants make it a garden. Plants lend color, texture, fragrance, form, and mass. Depending on how they're placed, they can bring focus to or deny a view. Plants can create a feeling of excitement or one of calm and serenity. They can shade us on sultry summer days or shield us from frigid winter winds.

With so many beautiful plants available, it's tempting to want them all. It's important to keep in mind, though, that a well-designed garden is more than a collection — it's a

Opposite: Phlox is a full-sun perennial that creates showy color in the garden. **Above:** Euphorbia is an easy perennial that thrives in poor soil.

Left: A confident hand with color can result in a border that provides interest all summer long. Below: A border of blue and yellow flowers forms an eye-catching combination. Opposite: Sedum, chrysanthemums, and coreopsis make a sizzling warm border.

coherent composition in which each plant complements the others and performs a specific function. Variety may be the spice of life, but in a garden too much variety may lead to indigestion.

One thing every southern gardener should do is take advantage of extended seasons. Too many people believe that gardening starts in March and ends in August. But the happy truth is, most of us can have something blooming outdoors in almost every month. And by planning ahead for upcoming seasons, we can create gardens that are wonderful to experience year-round.

Gardening with Color

Color is the garden's indispensable ingredient. Color has the power to thrill, attract, inspire, pacify, and awe. Consequently, most people equate color with beauty. They think the more color a scene has, the more beautiful it is, no matter what colors are used. But experienced gardeners know this just isn't so. Colors must work together. Colors splashed haphazardly around the yard looks less like a garden and more like a garish mistake.

To understand how colors work, gardeners must comprehend the vocabulary of color.

Contrasting colors (often called "complementary" colors) lie directly opposite each other on the color wheel. Examples include red and green, yellow and purple, and blue and orange. Contrasting colors make each other look brighter and naturally attract the eye. Adding a close neighbor of one of these contrasting colors — for example, blue and orange with blue's neighbor, blue-violet — makes a pleasing combination.

Warm colors consist of red, orange, yellow, and the colors in between. Visible from a distance, these colors enliven and energize a scene. Therefore, they make excellent accents and focal points. Against a neutral background, they pair well with one another. As individual colors, each goes well with blue.

Opposite: A border of white, pale blue, and violet delphiniums makes the most of the cool palette. **Below:** Yellow and purple flowers form a classically successful border.

Cool colors include blue, purple, green, and the colors in between. Many garden designers place white here, too, although purists might argue that white represents the absence of color. Cool colors quiet the garden. They create feelings of peace and serenity. They also serve as effective mediators between clashing colors such as orange and fuchsia.

Fifteen or twenty years ago, flower borders planned almost exclusively around cool colors were the rage. But times have changed, and so have tastes. Today many gardeners feel that cool-color-only gardens are boring. Such borders also tend to fade out in the dim light of early morning and late afternoon. The solution is to work in warmer colors.

Colorful Beginnings

Before you settle on a palette of colors, think for just a minute about where you live. Do you live in the city or in the suburbs? In the mountains or along the coast? In the Garden District of New Orleans or in the Buckhead section of Atlanta? Where you live does affect what colors people consider appropriate. For example, people at the beach paint their houses lavender, lemon yellow, and aquamarine and no one bats an eye. But try this in River Oaks in Houston and you might find yourself the subject of a petition. So choose colors that not only reflect your preferences and personality but also complement the setting around you.

Color Combinations That Work

As the adage goes, beauty is in the eye of the beholder. Some gardeners think certain combinations work magnificently; others think they look terrible. Still, when we examine the classic mixed borders of such famous gardens as Sissinghurst, Hidcote Manor, and Dumbarton Oaks, we can take a cue from their success. The following combinations work almost every time:

- blue, pink, and white
- bronze and chartreuse
- yellow and purple
- red, white, and green
- anything with blue

Combinations to avoid? Unless you're a brave soul, give a wide berth to pink and orange, pink and yellow, and red and pink. Of course, you can always smooth the waters by combining each pair with a transitional color that blends both colors. For example, try salmon flowers between pink and orange ones.

Annuals

The first key to mastering annuals is to get over the fact that they don't come back every year. True, you have to replant them, but they offer much in return. For one thing, they come in just about every color you can think of. For another, most of them bloom like crazy from the time you plant them until the time you pull them up months later. And when they finally give up the ghost, your garden begins anew. You get the chance to plant something totally different.

Annuals are classified as either cool-weather or warm-weather, depending on the type of conditions they prefer in order to grow and flower. Cool-weather annuals go into the ground in the fall (and sometimes in early spring). They survive freezing temperatures; bloom in cool, mild weather; and finally die when the hot weather arrives. Pansies, violas, English daisies, pot marigold *(calendula)*, sweet William, larkspur, and Shirley poppies are good examples. Warm-weather annuals are planted in spring and die with fall's first hard frost. They include

Use the following techniques when planning color for your garden:

- Repeat favorite colors throughout a garden to establish continuity and draw your eye from section to section.

- Place warm colors in the distance to call attention to garden ornament, destination, or focal point.

- Use cool colors near sitting areas to give them a feeling of peacefulness and intimacy.

- Make liberal use of plants with flowers or foliage of white, silver, gray, green, chartreuse, bronze, or deep purple. These plants help keep the peace between colors that don't like each other, such as yellow and pink.

Opposite: Caladiums and impatiens make great combinations in the shade garden. **Below right:** A curving expanse of hostas edged with pansies leads the eye into the garden. **Below left:** Zinnias add color to the garden and produce flowers for cutting all summer.

such popular flowers as impatiens, marigolds, waxleaf begonias, zinnias, and ageratum.

Naturally, some plants balk at being easily classified. Some cool-weather annuals are really perennials that can't take the South's hot summers. Good examples include delphiniums, lupines, and snapdragons. And some warm-weather annuals (such as pentas, coleus, and Mexican heather) are actually long-lived perennials where it doesn't freeze in winter. Bulbs throw another monkey wrench into the works. We treat hybrid tulips as annuals in the South because they don't like our mild winters. And most southerners treat caladiums as annuals because our mild winters still aren't mild enough for them.

Because annuals come in such variety, you'd be hard-pressed to think of all the ways you

could use them in the garden. You can mass them in large, formal beds for maximum impact; plant them in long, curving sweeps to lead visitors through a garden; or place them strategically throughout the garden in pots, hanging baskets, and window boxes. Don't forget to add annuals to mixed borders — they'll supply consistent color when the perennials are resting. Also add annuals to specialty gardens that often need extra color or underplanting, such as rose beds and vegetable gardens.

Don't be timid when setting out annuals. Plant them in groups of at least six or more for greater impact. Annuals come in market packs, so this isn't as expensive as it sounds. In most cases, you should plant in blocks of a single color, rather than mixing everything up.

179

Great Annuals for Anyone

Charlie Thigpen, associate garden editor for *Southern Living*, knows and grows more annuals than common sense allows. Here are his top ten easy-to-grow annuals for the South.

1. Narrowleaf zinnia (*Zinnia angustifolia*)
2. Lantana (perennial in mild winter areas)
3. Impatiens
4. Pansies and violas

5. Caladium
6. Spider flower (*Cleome*)
7. Dragonwing begonia
8. Cosmos

9. Coleus
10. Texas sage (*Salvia coccinea*)

Below: Successful perennial borders include plants that range in height, from tall spires to low, spreading plants.

However, some annuals, such as large-flowered zinnias, impatiens, bachelor's buttons, and Shirley poppies, look great in a color mix.

As mentioned earlier (page 175), some colors just work well together. But don't overlook the added appeal created by combining flowers of different shapes. For example, pair the vertical spikes of purple loosestrife (*Lythrum*) with the rounded, dinner-plate-size blooms of rose mallow (*Hibiscus moscheutos*).

Perennials

Someone once said, "A perennial is any plant that, had it lived, would have come back year after year." This observation is funny, but it also conveys the notion that perennials are somehow hard to grow. Nothing could be further from the truth. Southerners have a wonderful wealth of perennials from which to choose that are both easy to grow and long-lived.

Of course, calling a plant a perennial doesn't mean it's perennial everywhere. Whether a plant comes back reliably depends largely on the climate. For instance, delphiniums and lupines are perennials in the upper South but are annuals elsewhere in the South. In the same vein, lantana, cannas, and four o'clocks are perennials in the lower South but are annuals in the upper South.

When planning a perennial border, it is wise to bear in mind a few points that experienced gardeners have learned the hard way. First, almost all perennials prefer loose, well-drained soil. If your soil is heavy, boggy, or compacted, till in plenty of organic matter, such as sphag-

Can't-Miss Perennials

For years, Liz Tedder in Newnan, Georgia, has tended one of the prettiest perennial gardens in the South. Maintaining her garden could be a nightmare, if she didn't concentrate on plants that don't need babying. Here are some sure-fire perennials that always work for her.

Balloon flower *(Platycodon)*   Catmint *(Nepeta)*   Daylily   Perennial salvia

Russian sage *(Perovskia)*   Sedum   Summer phlox
(Phlox paniculata)

Right: A glorious rose reigns over a perennial bed of salvia and allium. Below: Hostas are a mainstay of the shade garden and come in a great variety, from variegated to glossy green leaves.

num peat moss, compost, and shredded bark. Or build a raised bed filled with good soil.

Second, remember that healthy perennials get bigger every year. Don't cram them too close together at first, or they may fill up the bed completely and crowd one another out. If the plant will eventually reach three feet wide, leave a space of at least eighteen inches on each side. If a plant gets too big, you can either move the plant to a new home or dig it up, divide into several plants, replant one of them, and give the rest away.

Third, don't be a purist. Relatively few perennials bloom continuously, so devoting a border to only perennials may mean enduring weeks at a time without any flowers. So it's a good idea to reserve space in your border for annuals. This way, even when perennials aren't

at their peak, you'll still have plenty of color.

Finally, don't overlook foliage. Plants such as cannas, hostas, ornamental grasses, lamb's ears, golden ray *(Ligularia)*, banana, and yucca often possess foliage that's as dynamic or more so than the flowers. And the foliage lasts a lot longer. Try mixing a coarsely leaved perennial, such as canna, with a finely leaved one, such as an ornamental grass. Contrasting textures brings life to a garden, even where there isn't a flower in sight.

Shade Gardening

Shade is a necessary evil in the southern garden. Big shade trees keep your house cooler and provide respite from the sun's glare, but they eliminate many hours of sunlight that plants like roses and perennials need. Still, there are bountiful choices of good plants to choose from when creating a shade garden. Keep in mind that shade conditions can vary, from the dappled light created by trees such as the honey locust, loblolly pine, and palms to the deep, even shade produced by magnolia and beech trees. In most cities in the lower and middle South, a shade garden proves to be much more appealing during hot summer

Popular Southern Shrubs

Azalea

Boxwood
(*Buxus sempervirens*
'Suffruticosa')

Common gardenia

Glossy abelia
(*Abelia grandiflora* 'Francis
Mason')

Oakleaf hydrangea

Butterfly bush

Spiraea bumalda

Rose (*Rosa* 'New Dawn')

Popular Shade Plants

Bear's breech (*Acanthus mollis*) Common foxglove Autumn fern Hosta

Lenten rose
(*Helleborus orientalis*) Plantain lily
(*Hosta* 'August Moon')

Japanese maple Oakleaf hydrangea Crape myrtle

Trees and Shrubs

Right: Crape myrtle provides summer color all over the South. Below: The oakleaf hydrangea is a staple in the southern garden, lending its graceful bulk to the landscape.

months than the exposed, Sahara-like conditions of an open, sunny space.

Some shade-loving plants that produce colorful blooms include native blue phlox (*Phlox divaricata*), white foamflowers (*Tiarella cordifolia*), Spanish bluebells, and hardy begonias.

Plant connoisseurs are especially fond of hostas and ferns. These shade-tolerant plants are a practical asset to a garden and provide the plant hunter countless opportunities to pursue rare varieties.

Shrubs

Shrubs are the defining element in a southern garden. The most perfect combination of flowering plants has little impact unless framed by shrubs chosen with care. Flowering shrubs,

like azaleas, create their own show in the spring and contribute to the colorful abundance of a cutting garden. Hydrangeas have the benefit of mop-headed, showy flowers along with a graceful limb habit and substantial leaves. Long after their blooms have faded, the oakleaf hydrangea contributes its delicate, papery blooms to the garden's texture. Keep in mind that hydrangeas bloom on old growth, so prune judiciously, removing only a few branches in late winter or early spring. Prune azaleas after they finish blooming.

Shrubs also serve to define the shape of a garden, directing the eye toward a focal point, enclosing a garden, and dividing it into clearly delineated areas. They can soften the lines of a house, connecting it to the garden. A piece of statuary framed by boxwood is highlighted like a diamond ring on a cushion of black velvet. Shrubs grown as tall hedges create privacy and are especially effective at keeping children and pets safely contained.

Shrubs can be pruned to complement any style of garden. A neatly clipped hedge accentuates a formal garden, while an unclipped buddleia, with its great arching branches, gives a free-spirited look to a blowzy border. Hollies

Vines

Wisteria (*Wisteria frutescens*)   Morning glory   Clematis (*Clematis armandii*)   Trumpet vine

Smilax (*Smilax lanceolata*)   Confederate jasmine   Carolina jessamine

pruned into tree forms add a formal touch. Left unpruned, they add substantial height to a garden, bridging the gap between the tree canopy and flower beds below.

Vines

Vines, with their romantic twining habit and tendency to dangle languorously, are a popular element in the southern garden. Some, like Confederate jasmine and smilax, seem to identify a garden as southern. They can perfume the air,

provide shade when trained over a pergola, and soften architectural features. Wisteria, perhaps the epitome of the southern vine, heralds the arrival of spring more reliably than any calendar.

Most vines need some form of support, and some, like the Lady Bank's rose, are so aggressive in their growth that they can nearly pull down a house. Wisteria sends out runners that allow the vine to become dangerously invasive. Steady maintenance and a set of sharp shears can keep vines in check.